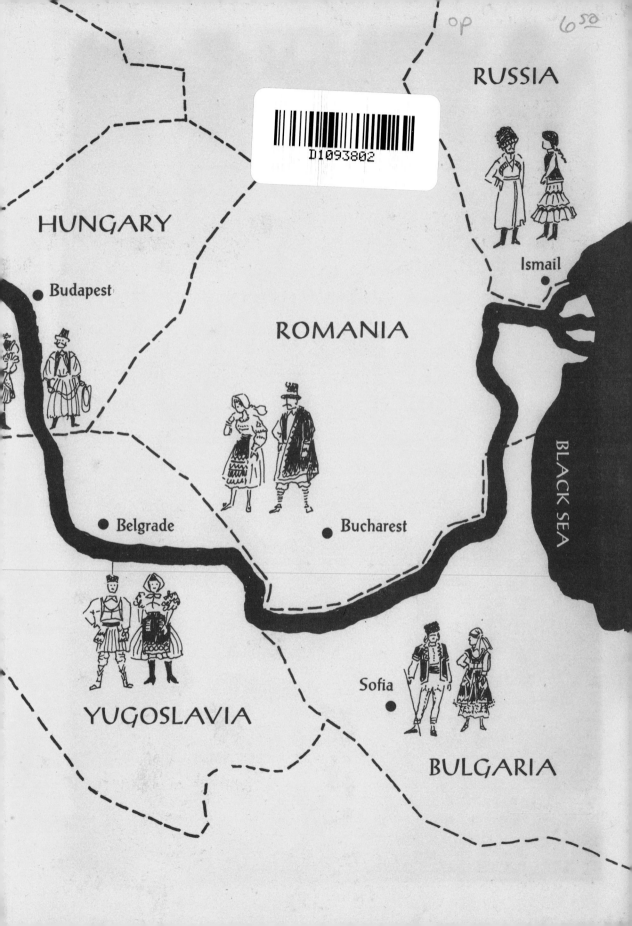

RUSSIA

HUNGARY

Budapest

ROMANIA

Ismail

Belgrade

Bucharest

BLACK SEA

YUGOSLAVIA

Sofia

BULGARIA

FOODS AND FESTIVALS OF THE DANUBE LANDS

Germany, Austria, Czechoslovakia, Hungary,
Yugoslavia, Bulgaria, Romania, Russia

By Lila Perl

FOODS AND FESTIVALS OF THE DANUBE LANDS
Germany, Austria, Czechoslovakia, Hungary,
Yugoslavia, Bulgaria, Romania, Russia

RICE, SPICE AND BITTER ORANGES
Mediterranean Foods and Festivals

RED-FLANNEL HASH AND SHOO-FLY PIE
American Regional Foods and Festivals

THE DELIGHTS OF APPLE COOKERY

WHAT COOKS IN SUBURBIA

[Illustrated by LEO GLUECKSELIG]

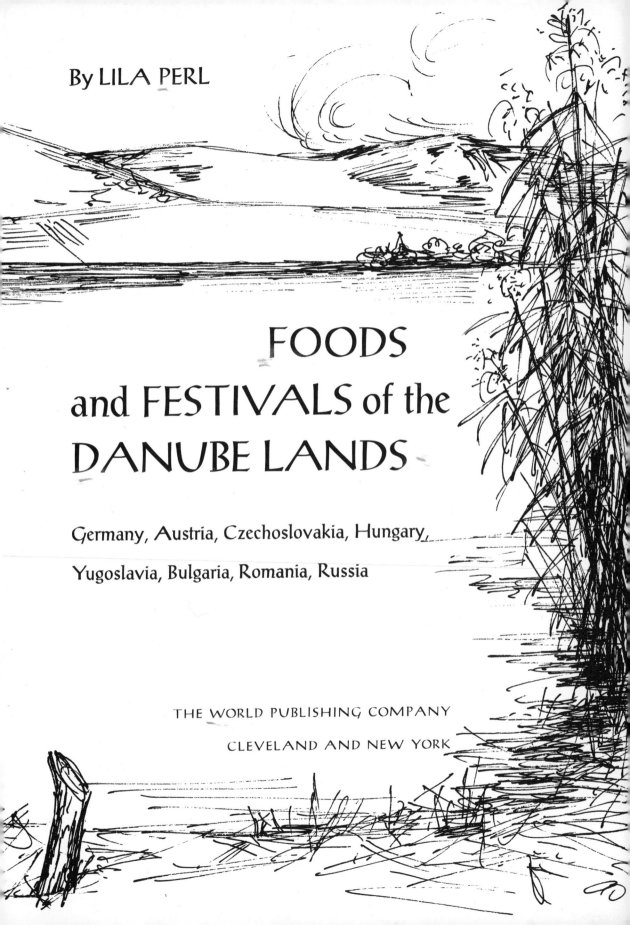

By LILA PERL

FOODS
and FESTIVALS of the
DANUBE LANDS

Germany, Austria, Czechoslovakia, Hungary,

Yugoslavia, Bulgaria, Romania, Russia

THE WORLD PUBLISHING COMPANY

CLEVELAND AND NEW YORK

Published by The World Publishing Company
2231 West 110th Street, Cleveland, Ohio 44102
Published simultaneously in Canada by
Nelson, Foster & Scott Ltd.
Library of Congress catalog card number: 69-13064
Text copyright © 1969 by Lila Perl
Illustrations copyright © 1969 by Leo Glueckselig
Designed by Jack Jaget

CONTENTS

8   CONTENTS

RECIPE CONTENTS

FOODS AND FESTIVALS OF THE DANUBE LANDS

Germany, Austria, Czechoslovakia, Hungary, Yugoslavia, Bulgaria, Romania, Russia

THE DANUBE

THE GYPSIES call it "the dustless road." Social scientists refer to it as a "highway of history." Geographers rank it the second longest river in Europe.

It begins as a trickling mountain spring in the *Schwarzwald*, the Black Forest of southwestern Germany. At this point it is a mere garden path of a river. Its destiny seems uncertain. It meanders, hesitates, stumbles onward, even disappears entirely for a while into a bed of reeds.

By the time it has traveled some seventy-five miles, it is still only a dirt road of a river, comfortable for canoes, rowboats, and very light cargo craft. But shortly before it leaves Germany to enter Austria, the river, swollen by other rivers rushing down on it from mountain sources, comes of age. From here on it is alternately broad-backed and regal, roiling and tempestuous, a splendid safe superhighway, a terrifying series of flashing dips and curves.

At the end of its exhausting eastward vagabondage the river meanders once again, not as a stumbling infant now but as a lazy giant made sluggish by its own might, pausing to survey its immense girth. Here near its mouth the river's domain is sixty miles wide. It zigzags through two thousand square miles of marshy delta and eases itself at last, by way of three main channels, into the Black Sea. On the opposite shore lies Asia.

The river's journey has taken it through or past eight countries of central and eastern Europe. In nearly each one of these countries the river has a different name. In Germany and Austria it is called the *Donau*; to Czechoslovaks it is the *Dunaj*. Hungarians call it the *Duna*; Yugoslavs and Bulgarians, the *Dunav*; Romanians, the *Dunărea*; and in Russian it is the *Dunay*. The ancient Romans called it the *Danubius*. We call it the Danube.

FROM THE BLACK FOREST TO THE BLACK SEA

At once we realize that the Danube world is made up of a variety of languages—four basically different language groups, seven separate tongues—as well as a large number of racial strains, half a dozen major world religions, a broad range of customs, traditions, and political viewpoints. As one might expect, many of these differences have caused severe disagreement and brought intense strife to the Danube lands over the centuries.

There is even disagreement as to the color of the Danube. Johann Strauss described it as being blue, possibly because the German word *blau* rhymes so well with *Donau*. Contrary to this pleasant and romantic Viennese viewpoint, the Danube is more often a muddy brown, for each year it carries away with it to the sea one hundred million tons of silt.

At other times the Danube is a steely gray, a murky green, an angry churning white, a soupy yellow. It is true of course that the Danube is sometimes blue. This is most likely to happen in its upper course while it is still a young river, sometime during the winter months before the melting snows have begun to wash down from the mountains. Lovers, of course, have always maintained that the Danube is blue.

Political observers detect still another color when they peer into Danubian waters. From Czechoslovakia eastward they have dubbed it the "red" Danube, for six of the eight

Danube countries are presently under some form of Communist-oriented government.

There are other color discrepancies in the Danube world. The Black Forest in which the Danube is born is not black, nor is it really a forest. It takes its name from the dark hue of the evergreens that cover its mountain slopes, but there are many sunny uplands and cleared pastoral valleys in the Black Forest, and the wooded areas are neither thick nor jungle-like, for there is surprisingly little undergrowth between the trees.

The Black Sea is another misnomer. In fair weather, and especially in summer, the pale sands of its rapidly developing coastal resorts melt into deep turquoise waters. The Turks are said to have given the Black Sea its name, the Turkish word being *Karadeniz.* The Turks were motivated not by the sight of dark-hued waters but rather by fear, for having migrated for centuries across the vast land mass of Asia they came at last to this sea and found its great size awesome.

It is true, of course, that the Black Sea is not as clear as the Mediterranean. But the silt that is deposited in it by the Danube and other rivers is largely nitrogen-enriched mud, making the Black Sea particularly inviting to a variety of excellent food fish.

It is a very ancient sea. In prehistoric times it was part of an immense landlocked body of fresh water. When the earth's crust folded, thrusting up the Caucasus Mountains, this sea was divided. The waters to the west of the mountains became the Black Sea; those to the east, the Caspian Sea. After the last ice age a channel formed, opening the way to the Mediterranean, and the Black Sea began to grow salty. Even today, however, it is less salty than the Mediterranean because of the mighty rivers that roll into it, among them the Dnieper, the Don, and of course the Danube.

The length of the Danube is still another matter for disagreement. Some geographers estimate it at 1,750 miles, some at 1,776 miles, and there are other figures cited that fall between these two. These variations are due to the river's erratic flow in places where it has cut multiple channels, particularly in the delta region. In any case, the Danube is second in length only to the Volga among European rivers. The Volga, however, is not an international stream. It flows entirely within the Soviet Union.

The word "delta" comes, of course, from the fourth letter of the Greek alphabet. Most great river mouths are shaped like this letter, in a triangle with one of the straight sides giving onto the sea into which the river flows. From the point directly opposite that side of the triangle, the river divides into numerous streams and usually several main channels.

The Danube delta, which is located in Romania and borders in the north on the Soviet Union, is a wondrous watery world of reed-grown marshes and tiny fishing villages, of floating islands and dim forests festooned with creepers and vines. It is one of the world's great bird sanctuaries and it is also the source of huge sturgeon that weigh close to 1,000 pounds and yield much of the world's finest caviar.

Through extensive damming, towns have been created in the Danube delta. Wheat and others crops are grown, and sheep and cattle find sufficient land for grazing. But life is never secure in these waterbound villages, for the river comes from a long way off and one never knows what it will bring with it. Disasters due to rising waters are common.

While delta floods are a constant menace, the Danube has also wreaked havoc much farther upstream. In the city of Budapest, through which the Danube cuts a wide swath, the winter of 1838 saw catastrophe. A severe ice jam caused the river to burst its banks, heaving icebergs into the streets, sweeping away thousands of buildings, and drowning some one thousand people.

The Danube is at its most tempestuous, however, in that narrow defile between Yugoslavia and Romania known as the Iron Gate. Swollen during its flow through Yugoslavia by the waters of the Tisza and the Drava, the Sava and the Morava, the Danube rolls heavily eastward. Suddenly its great power is compressed. The river hurls itself into a two-mile-long passageway, a corridor of rock formed by the southward-dipping Carpathians and the northerly-arching

Balkan Mountains. The precipitous cliffs that hold the river in their grip drop 2,000 feet to the water's edge. The river boils and lashes as it tumbles over its boulder-strewn bed.

For centuries downstream voyages were hazardous even when the river was high. Upstream voyages were impossible. Upon reaching the Iron Gate region, cargo had to be unloaded, carried overland, and put aboard other ships that waited beyond the danger point. The original craft returned to their downstream ports. Not until 1896, after a six-year blasting project, was the river widened at the Iron Gate and a deepened ship channel cleared of rocks created, thus making safe navigation possible in both directions.

One wonders how the legions of ancient Rome were able to penetrate the Iron Gate region in the first century A.D., a time when the Danube was considered the northern boundary of the empire and of the civilized Western world. The answer is written in the sheer-faced rock walls on the Yugoslav side of the Danube. Looking up, one can see today the narrow ledge that the Romans carved out of the cliffside, and the Roman mortise holes into which stout beams were fitted at right angles, extending outward over the water.

These beams became the subsurface of a wood-planked road, thus broadening the ledge into a highway suspended in space. On this military highway, which ran for about twelve miles through the gorge, the armies of the Emperor Trajan advanced into Romania, then known as Dacia. Although it took Roman engineers and Roman labor forces more than half a century to complete it, Trajan's Road (as it has been known throughout history) was perhaps the most striking achievement of a people who were no mean roadbuilders.

Although its timbers have long since rotted away, Trajan's Road also attests to the power Rome exercised over the ancient world. Rome was never really able to establish authority in the central European barbarian strongholds north of the Danube; yet she reached for the province of Dacia to the east, took it, and held it until A.D. 271.

It is because of this that the people of Romania, although they are surrounded chiefly by Slavic-speaking peoples, today speak a Latin-based Romance tongue. The Romanians are proud of their Roman heritage and prefer that the English spelling of their country's name reflect this—thus Romania rather than Rumania or Roumania.

The Danube was a "highway of history" even for people less ingenious than the Romans. If they could not sail its waters or scale its cliffs, they followed it closely by a land route, for the Danube's west-east flow is almost unique among European rivers. Originating in the Occident and flowing toward the Orient, the Danube was the pathway that in prehistoric times beckoned the New Stone Age civilization of the Middle East toward Europe.

Later it was to beckon wave upon wave of wild horsemen from the Asian steppes—Attila and the Huns in the fifth

century A.D., the Magyars who settled Hungary late in the ninth century, the Mongols who conquered Russia and swept on farther west in the thirteenth century, and the Turks who twice threatened Vienna after they took Constantinople in 1453, and who continued to occupy parts of eastern Europe into the twentieth century.

The Danube, of course, has been a two-way highway. The Romans, as we have seen, used it to extend the long arm of the empire into eastern Europe and to implant an island of Latin-based culture there. In the 800s Charlemagne used the Danube to extend the domains of his Frankish empire, thus laying the basis for the Holy Roman Empire. The Crusaders in the 1100s and 1200s and Napoleon in the

1800s followed the Danube land route as they pressed eastward.

History is tightly intertwined with legend along a river as old as the Danube. Like the Rhine, the Danube has its Lorelei, its river maiden who sits upon a perilous rock, singing and idly combing her silken tresses. The Danubian Lorelei is named Isa; she waits to beguile the unwary sailor and to destroy his craft along a stretch of the river in Austria which is a tortuous passageway near where the wine-growing Wachau district begins.

Farther downstream along Austria's castle-studded Danubian shores is the ancient fortress of Dürnstein. Here the English king Richard the Lion-Hearted, returning from a crusade to the Holy Land in 1192, was imprisoned by his enemy, Duke Leopold of Austria.

Blondel, Richard's confidential servant and favorite minstrel, went in search of his master. At this point history fuses into legend. It is said that the faithful Blondel sang outside the castle walls of half of Europe until he learned by chance that a prisoner of rank languished in the gloomy keep of Dürnstein on Austria's middle Danube. Arriving at the castle at last, Blondel placed himself below the iron grating of the tower walls and began to sing a French lay he had composed for Richard. The king, hearing his minstrel's voice, responded singing the same song.

Overjoyed, Blondel returned to England and obtained the ransom that led to King Richard's release. The ransom sum was a very large one and the enterprising Austrians used the money—this part of the story is established as fact—to build the city walls of Vienna. It was those very same walls that served in 1529 and again in 1683 to repel the Turks during their long, fierce sieges of Vienna.

STONE AGE MAN IN THE DANUBE LANDS

Stranger than any Danubian legend is the slowly curving course of history. A glance backward into the shadowy eons of prehistory helps us to trace man's progress from hunting to husbandry, from root grubbing to cereal growing. For it

was this transition, which took place at the beginning of the
New Stone Age (about 6000 B.C.), that established the
earliest civilizations and made possible the great variety of
national and regional cuisines that the world knows today.

But to understand how that moment came to be when
man put the first seed in the ground and nurtured it, we
must go back a few thousand more years to the Old Stone
Age.

The closing centuries of the Old Stone Age coincided with
the end of the great ice age known as the Pleistocene Epoch.
This was an era that brought gradual but startling changes
to Danubian Europe. By about 8000 B.C. the earth's climate
had begun to grow warm once again and the ice cap that
covered northern Europe started its retreat toward the polar
region.

What had long been semifrozen plains, a kind of Siberian

tundra in central Europe, were now transformed into temperate-zone forest lands. The old animal inhabitants—the bison, the reindeer, the woolly mammoth—began to vanish. Some migrated to plains areas in more northerly latitudes where their species continued to thrive; other species like the woolly mammoth were doomed to extinction.

It is interesting to note that whole specimens of this furred ice-age elephant have been found in modern times in Siberia, solidly frozen and fantastically well preserved from Pleistocene times. Even more remarkable perhaps is the courage of those scientists who in 1912 attended a banquet in St. Petersburg where mammoth meat was served. The animal whose flesh was sampled had been taken from nature's freezer near the mouth of Siberia's Lena River. None of the diners reported any serious aftereffects.

With the disappearance of the ice age animals from central Europe, animals that could adapt to forest living began to appear—the deer and the elk, the wild boar, and the smaller woodland animals such as foxes, martens, and beavers. It was the dawn of the Middle Stone Age; its people, who now developed the bow and arrow for more efficient forest hunting, became known to history as the "forest folk."

In southern Europe similar climate and scenery changes had taken place as a result of the decline of the ice age. But the forests of the Mediterranean fringe lands were later to be denuded by man and prevented from self-renewal by the feeding habits of goats and sheep. In central Europe the lush forests were to maintain themselves and to endure in surprisingly large areas into modern times.

As the lakes and rivers of central Europe warmed, man took to spear fishing and to shellfish gathering along the muddy shores. An abundance of meat and fish led to thoughts of preserving food for future use, and now Danubian man began to dry shreds and strips of flesh by smoking them over a fire or by baking them in the heat of the sun.

The forests offered other foods—nuts and berries, roots and shoots, tasty new grubs and insects, wild honey, pleasant fresh herbs. The Middle Stone Age was kind to Danubian man. His range of foods was expanding. His diet was much more varied and satisfying than that afforded by the chilly barren grass plains of the Old Stone Age. But of course he still only *collected* his food by shooting, spearing, picking, or gathering; he did nothing about *producing* the food he ate.

The Middle Stone Age was less benevolent in other parts of the world than it was in Europe. In western Asia, for example, something odd had taken place along with the decline of the ice age. The change in the earth's climate had brought a new set of precipitation patterns to the world, and in the Middle East the weather was becoming dryer and dryer.

As centuries passed and the aridity of the once fertile plateaus intensified, men and animals collected closer to the major water sources: the Indus River valley in what is now West Pakistan, the Tigris-Euphrates valley in what is now Iraq, and the Nile delta.

Here, in fairly stable primitive communities, the miracle of plant life could be carefully observed. Man watched the growth cycle of the wild cereal grasses, those crude varieties of wheat and barley that he gathered for food. Soon he was sowing the seed himself, expanding the crop, selecting the better kinds of grasses for propagation.

The animals that left the increasingly barren plateaus of western Asia also sought the watering places, and it was here that man turned to large-scale herding. Wild strains of cattle, sheep, and swine were domesticated. The New Stone Age (Neolithic Period) had evolved. Man had turned from hunting and food gathering to animal herding and agriculture.

He would still pursue the hunt, however, to round out his food requirements. There would even be wild-boar hunts and stag hunts in the royal hunting preserves of Austria and Bavaria in the well-fed 1880s. But man—at least in the Neolithic communities of western Asia—no longer depended entirely on what he could spear, stone, grapple with, or find growing wild and rip out of the ground.

By 3000 B.C. the settled, food-producing communities of southwestern Asia had grown markedly in population. More people meant that more food had to be grown and raised, and more food in turn increased the size of the population. Fertile new lands were clearly required for farming and

herding. Pretty soon the cry went up for living space, just as the cry for *Lebensraum* went up in the very heart of Europe in the twentieth century. But in Neolithic times it represented the need for farming land; in Nazi Germany of the 1930s this demand was designed to burst the national borders for broad economic and political purposes.

In any case, groups of people began to splinter off from the clustered, land-poor communities of the Middle East. They trekked slowly westward toward the Black Sea and the Mediterranean. With them they carried the seeds of cereal grains and legumes, and with them came their herds of livestock.

Once they had reached the Black Sea region, many followed a route directly up the Danube basin. Others kept to the southern coast of Europe and then bore north, for frequently their destination was the European heartland. New Neolithic communities were beginning to appear in the Swiss lake regions and in the German Rhineland, in Austria at Lake Hallstatt, in France, Sweden, Holland, and northern Italy. Food-producing man had arrived in Europe.

The Bronze Age (about 1500 B.C. to 1000 B.C. in Danubian Europe) saw the rapid development of that pork-and-dumpling, beer-and-black-bread cuisine that we associate with the Danube lands today.

TOWARD A DANUBIAN CUISINE

In southern Europe other influences were at work. Differences of climate, soil, and terrain, and the presence of the Mediterranean seacoast, were making for a different cuisine, one that was based on fish and olive oil, on wheaten bread and wine.

From the start cereals had been the mainstay of the

Danubian agricultural communities. Cereals were the source of bread and beer. Wheat, barley, buckwheat, oats, and rye were grown. Emmer wheat, the type originally cultivated in Egypt and in the Tigris-Euphrates valley, was a crude bread wheat better suited to porridge. But it was used, as was barley, for the unleavened bread cakes that were being baked in Germany possibly as late as 800 B.C., at which time leavened bread became more widely known north of the Danube.

It was in ancient Egypt that leavened bread had been discovered many centuries earlier. Soon afterward barley lost its popularity as a bread grain in the land of the Nile, for barley contains little or no gluten and makes for a crumbly rather than a pleasantly elastic raised loaf. The Egyptians turned to the development of the better bread wheats. But barley continued to be popular as a source of beer, which the early Egyptians prepared from fermented half-baked barley bread.

In Danubian Europe, too, barley fell off as a bread grain once raised loaves were introduced. But the preference for dark, coarse-grained breads was deeply established and has continued into the present. And of course the cultivation of barley continued for its use as porridge and in soups, and especially for its malt extract used in brewing beer.

Rye flour is an extremely popular ingredient in Danubian breads. The origin of rye is rather obscure. It is believed, along with oats, to be a weed closely resembling wheat that sprang up in wheatfields in the early days of agriculture. Botanists call such a plant a "mimic contaminant."

Buckwheat, another favorite cereal grain of the Danube lands, especially in eastern Europe, is extremely hardy. It is easy to grow even in areas that skirt Arctic regions as it requires a short growing season. This accounts for its popularity in Russia, where it is used for a porridge known as *kasha* and for a somewhat coarse flour that gives special flavor to the Russian pancakes called *blini*.

In any case, it is difficult to imagine a Danubian country without its loaf of thick-crusted, chewy rye bread, often flecked with caraway seeds, or its moist, nutty-flavored dark-brown pumpernickel or black bread.

The prevalence of this basic food tradition is in part due to the lack of Roman influence throughout much of Danubia. The Romans not only planted grapevines wherever they developed colonies (including Britain, where the climate soon proved unfavorable), but they also established the practice of eating bread baked of white wheaten flour. Wheat was grown in almost every corner of the far-flung Roman empire and it was milled into a highly refined bread flour.

If we look at countries like France, Spain, Italy, and Greece today, the Roman wine-and-white-bread tradition does seem deeply embedded. But the barbaric lands north of the Danube that never came under Roman sway certainly appear to have followed a beer-and-black-bread tradition.

White-bread eaters have always shown a certain snobbishness toward black-bread eaters. The Scythians, a nomadic tribe of the Black Sea region, were regarded as barbaric by the ancient Greeks with whom they traded, principally because they ate oats. The Greeks simply did not regard oats as anything but cattle feed. And Alexandre Dumas in his *Great Dictionary of Cuisine*, published in 1873 after his death, could not as a true Frenchman resist a swipe at the German pumpernickel.

"The name is derived," says Dumas in a brazenly made-up

story, "from the exclamation of a horseman who, after tasting it, gave the rest to his horse, whose name was Nick, saying, 'Bon pour Nick!' [Good for Nick], which, with the German accent, became *Pompernick*."

The forestation of Danubian Europe, which took place at the end of the Old Stone Age, brought one of the most valuable food animals to that part of the world—the hog. The hog is not a grass-eating animal but rather a forest and swamp animal with a strong preference for roots, nuts, and flesh. Nomadic peoples have seldom kept swine, for unlike sheep and cattle, they cannot be driven long distances.

But the settled forest and lake dwellings of late Neolithic times in Europe attracted wild hogs, especially as the garbage heaps grew up around these communities. Swine are natural scavengers and although the Hebrews, the ancient Egyptians, and later the Moslems all rejected the pig as food, the Danubian peoples readily risked trichinosis, tapeworm, and other diseases for the sake of gaining such an easily domesticated and valuable food animal.

Often a weak or defective wild hog became the nucleus of a relatively amenable herd. Soon Danubian man was a pig farmer. It was not a long way from here to dishes like the pigs' knuckles and sauerkraut of Germany or the roast pork with bread dumplings of Czechoslovakia.

Just as the growing of cereals in Danubian Europe meant

that legumes, root crops, and other vegetables were also being grown, so both cattle and sheep, in addition to swine, were being gathered into herds. The Neolithic peoples who migrated to Europe often brought the tamed descendants of wild sheep with them, and cattle descended from wild oxen were to be found in both southwestern Asia and in Europe.

Now that man was living in permanent communities and becoming skilled at crop growing, he could provide an ample food supply for his animals as well as himself. And a manageable herd meant more than a handy meat supply—it meant a ready source of milk and milk products. Just as the Tartars of central Asia drank mare's milk and the tundra people close to the Arctic Circle drank reindeer milk, the Neolithic folk of Europe drank the milk of cows, sheep, and goats.

In northern and central Europe it was possible to make butter, since milk could be kept fresh for the many hours required for the cream to rise. In southern Europe, however, where milk soured more rapidly, it was better to make the milk into cheese, which keeps for long periods. It is easy to see why olive oil became the "butter" of the Mediterranean lands while butter became an important flavoring and cooking ingredient in the Danube lands.

In the Swiss lake dwellings of the late Neolithic period, the basic foods were cereals and vegetables, meats and dairy products, and fish. We also know that the lake dwellers made cider from wild apples and that they fermented wild berries into a kind of wine. For a sweetener they gathered wild honey and they were even producing such flavoring ingredients as caraway and poppy seed, which are widely used in central Europe today. Imagine a kaiser roll without its coating of poppy seeds or a steaming dish of sauerkraut or stewed cabbage without caraway seeds!

Carrots, beans, and lentils as well as wheat and barley were cultivated in nearby fields. The bread of the lake dwellers was unleavened. The lake dwellings themselves were supported by stilts and were built out over the water along the lake shores. The houses were constructed of wood and were usually rectangular. The piles that supported the lake houses were firmly planted in the mud and were held in place by heaps of rocks. Wooden platforms ran around each house or cluster of houses. Some houses are believed to have had a trap door through which fish could be speared or caught in a net. Food was regularly dropped or dangled into the water in order to attract the fish.

The first discovery of the remains of a prehistoric lake-dwelling community took place in 1853 at a lake near Zurich. Along with weapons and tools of bone, horn, and metal, pottery vessels were found which contained fruit and grain. All of these were well preserved by the mud of the lake bottom.

Pottery making had developed rapidly in Neolithic times because it was necessary to have containers in which to store milk, grain, and other products. Pottery or other hollow ware was essential, too, for beer brewing and cereal making. Thus, while people of the Old and Middle Stone Ages did most of their cooking by roasting food over an open fire, New Stone Age man had begun to use vessels for some of his cooking.

There were only a few basic foodstuffs that had not yet arrived in central Europe by the end of the Bronze Age. Chickens, which are descended from the wild jungle fowl of India and which were first domesticated in that country, did not reach the Mediterranean world until 600 B.C. It was much later when this type of poultry became generally known farther north. But waterfowl had been abundant in Danubian Europe from early times—and there is still a marked preference for ducks and geese throughout this area. Even gulls' eggs are extremely well liked in northern Germany, just as in prehistoric times.

Fruit culture remained very limited north of the Danube even after the onset of the Roman era with its accent on fruit growing in the colonial lands. Although the Swiss lake dwellers had apples, they were primitive varieties, small, hard, and sour. As to spices and seasonings, it was not until the development of the sea trade in the Middle Ages that many important flavoring accents came into Danubian cuisine.

Trade did exist, however, during the Danubian Bronze Age. Two very important articles of trade were amber and salt. Salt had been especially vital to mankind since the dawn of the Neolithic era with its development of agriculture, for a diet that includes cereals and legumes produces greater salt hunger than does a diet consisting largely of meats and fish. Salt, obtained by mining or by evaporating it from the sea, was exchanged for other items of value from the very beginning of the Neolithic era in Europe.

Amber, although of far less practical value, was a highly prized article of trade in Bronze Age Europe. Amber, which is formed naturally from the resins of pine trees, was found in large deposits in the Baltic Sea region and was transported from there to Greece by Scandinavian traders. Ancient peoples believed that amber had magic properties because when it was rubbed with cloth or fur it developed static electricity and would attract bits of straw, hair, or other lightweight substances.

The Greeks set great value on the possession of an amulet polished from a chunk of this hard, yellow-brown, semi-

transparent material. They called amber *elektron* because of what they considered to be its life-giving quality. It is from this Greek word that the word "electricity" is derived.

The Danes and other Scandinavian traders who made the long land trek south with their amber returned with articles of bronze from the culturally more advanced Mediterranean world. But by about 1000 B.C. another metal began to replace bronze in Greece, just as weapons and tools of bronze (an alloy of copper and tin) had at one time supplanted those of stone. Now the traders returning from the Mediterranean introduced implements of iron to the farming folk of the Danube lands. Thus, between 1000 and 900 B.C., the Bronze Age began to give way to the Iron Age in central Europe.

The smelting and forging of iron was discovered in Asia Minor about 1100 B.C., and the knowledge of how to handle this cheap and abundant metal soon reached Greece. In central Europe agriculture in particular benefited from the Iron Age as crop production was increased through the development of an iron plow.

Had the relatively peaceful farming folk of Danubian Europe maintained their pastoral existence until the era of Roman conquest, Rome would undoubtedly have had an even larger empire, and central and eastern Europe might today bear the strong stamp of Latin culture and Mediterranean civilization.

But in the two hundred years or so preceding the birth of Christ, Germanic tribes began to filter south from the North Sea and Baltic regions. These semisavage folk, at first from Denmark and northern Germany, later from Sweden and other parts of Scandinavia, were driven toward central Europe by overpopulation, by prolonged periods of flooding, by the migratory instincts of a semiagricultural people who still depended largely on hunting. Also, being warlike, they required a great deal of *Lebensraum*, large areas of no man's land between tribal groups, to prevent the constant warfare that sometimes thinned their ranks to the vanishing point.

These Germanic tribes, later augmented by tribes of nomadic horsemen from Asia, formed a seething mass of barbarians north of the Danube that Roman armies could not subdue. The barbarians were to ransack Rome itself many times and were to survive the decline of the Roman Empire.

It is true that Danubian man of the Roman era did not seem very promising in terms of contributing an advanced culture or a spirit of enlightenment to world civilization. And in the centuries since then he has sometimes appeared to revert to his former savagery. Nevertheless the Danube lands have been responsible for a high order of achievement in areas ranging from science and technology to philosophy, music, and the other arts.

Their folklore is as brilliant as their history is turbulent. Their cuisine ranges from bland to fiery; it embraces elements of Western homeliness and heartiness piqued with the exotic and subtle flavors of the East. Each Danube land has its special quality that is a distillation of its geography,

its history, and its mixture of peoples reacting in that particular setting.

To know the Danube world one must embark upon a downstream journey on the river that links its diverse lands and people. Choose your craft—a homely cargo barge or a handsome passenger steamer brimming with holiday makers; a fragile, solitary canoe in which to challenge the river's overwhelming expanse and fearsome patches of white water, or a gleaming hydrofoil that skims the surface at fifty miles an hour.

Few can resist the Danube, for it is a river that captures the imagination, a river that runs through the heartland of Europe to the shores of Asia like a glistening thread through a tapestry.

GERMANY

THERE IS scarcely a place name in Germany that does not evoke the sight, smell, and taste of some appetite-arousing food. The cities of Hamburg and Frankfurt, sources of the grilled meat patty and the sizzling hotdog, are perhaps the most obvious. But there are many more.

The city of Braunschweig says liver sausage, mellow and lightly spiced; Düsseldorf says mustard. The historic region of Westphalia is almost synonymous with the thin-sliced, richly flavored raw ham it produces, and with its equally flavorful dark pumpernickel. Holstein, in the north, is schnitzel, a breaded, fried veal slice, with a fried egg on top and a garnish of anchovies and capers.

Münster and Limburg waft their rare perfumes of cheese. Even famous people do not escape the association with some form of delicatessen. Bismarck, the "iron chancellor," champion of German unity, is a herring, sharp and salty, pickled in onions, vinegar, and hot red peppers.

A Bismarck can also mean a jelly doughnut in Germany, especially among Berliners whose city lies in what was once Bismarck's Prussia. Nuremberg makes one think of gingery frosted *Lebkuchen*, Dresden of fruit-studded Christmas *Stollen*. One could go on and on. Germany appears to be a vast purveyor of delicatessen and bakery goods, sausage maker and gingerbread baker to the world.

Having nibbled at place names scattered across the length and breadth of Germany—north and south with their regional variations, east and west with their political differences—one begins to think a bit about the shape of this land situated at the very core of Europe.

Asked to draw a map of Germany from memory, few people can come up with anything close to accuracy. Germany is not Italy, Spain, France, or the British Isles. The one thing certain about Germany is that it is "in the middle."

One reason for this haziness about the shape of Germany is that Germany did not exist as a nation until the last half of the nineteenth century. It was simply a conglomeration of smallish kingdoms, duchies, baronies, and principalities. Some of these were merely city-states, a few square miles in area. In the sixteenth century there were over three hundred capital cities in Germany.

Another reason for uncertainty about Germany's borders is that since 1871 Germany's shape has undergone marked changes every so many years. Germany reminds one of a rather stout woman who keeps going on a diet. Suddenly she has a brand new figure; now she is plump again; now she is trimmer than ever.

Between 1871 and 1914, the years of growing German imperialism, first under Count Otto von Bismarck and later under Kaiser Wilhelm II, Germany was a large sprawling mass with tentacles reaching northward into Denmark and dipping eastward into Poland and Russia.

After World War I, Germany shrank considerably and had one of her tentacles lopped off in order to give Poland an outlet to the Baltic Sea, known as the Polish Corridor. But in 1933 Adolf Hitler came on the scene and by 1939 he had fattened Germany to a pudgy roundness by annexing Austria and western Czechoslovakia. All the hollows and gaunt spots that had resulted from Germany's defeat in World War I were filled out and Germany was poised for conquest.

Defeat in World War II was even more disastrous than

in World War I. Since 1945 Germany has been at her slimmest since before the days of unification. Her waist is nipped in by France on the west and Czechoslovakia on the east; Austria and Poland are re-established as independent countries; and if one slices away the nearly one third of territory within German borders that constitutes East Germany, West Germany is indeed a mere slip of a girl compared to the blowzy *Hausfrau* of former days.

Despite this reduction in girth, Germany is eating better than ever. Her cuisine is at its most varied and plentiful, her beer halls are crowded into the small hours, her pre-Lenten *Fasching* (*Karneval* or carnival) is a time of the richest eating anywhere, and her *Oktoberfest* is at its most rollicking. Robust is probably the word that best describes Germany's foods and festivals, for they are the by-products of a lusty and expansive history.

"All have fierce blue eyes, red hair, huge frames. . . ." **DAILY LIFE OF THE**

We are indebted to Tacitus, the Roman historian who **GERMANIC TRIBES** lived from about A.D. 55 to 117, for much of what we know about the semicivilized Germanic tribes that inhabited central Europe during the Roman era.

Julius Caesar, who conquered Britain and Gaul but could not subdue those peoples who lived east of the Rhine and north of the Danube, also wrote about the barbarians who were such a source of frustration to his armies. The tribes themselves were for the most part illiterate and left few records of their civilization aside from their tombs and some hand implements.

They built no cities and continued their preference for living in crude villages set well apart from one another, as tribal groups and even as family groups within the tribes. Their country, Tacitus wrote, "either bristles with forests or reeks with swamps." Their land "is productive of grain, but unfavorable to fruit-bearing trees; it is rich in flocks and herds, but they are for the most part undersized. . . ." Dwellings were built of timber and were "rude masses without ornament or attractiveness."

The men of the Germanic tribes were "fit only for a sudden exertion." According to Tacitus, who used both eye-witness and written reports for his *Germania*, they preferred hunting and fighting to more laborious work. They dressed in animal skins, worked both leather and metal which they employed as fighting garb, and wielded spears, swords, and battle-axes of metal and stone. Although many of their acts bordered on savagery, the Germanic peoples were not savages. They were barbarians, meaning a foreign and only half-civilized people as viewed by the Greeks and Romans of antiquity.

Between 200 B.C. and A.D. 500, Germanic peoples in bewildering numbers massed across the face of Europe in a kind of restless reshufflement. Each tribal group seemed destined for some part of Europe other than its place of origin. Most of the tribes came from northern Europe and were dubbed "Germanic" by the Romans, and from this the country of Germany later received its name. Many of them settled permanently in that country, but often a tribe would split, some moving on to other lands. Thus, a people who came from Denmark and most of whom ended up in Italy, or a people who originated in Sweden and swept through Spain into Africa, were also labeled Germanic.

The Teutones or Teutoni were one of the first of the

Germanic groups to migrate south. From their home near the mouth of the Elbe River in northern Germany they moved toward Roman territory and constituted a threat to Rome as early as 102 B.C. The Teutones gave their name to the Teutonic languages which include German, Dutch, Flemish, English, and most Scandinavian tongues.

Later came the Alemanni, who occupied territory along the Rhine and were to provide the French with their name for Germany, *l'Allemagne*. The Franks, still another Germanic tribe, defeated the Alemanni, moved farther west, and gave France its name. The Saxons migrated from Denmark to Germany and westward to northern Gaul. From there they raided the coast of Britain and in the sixth century, along with the Jutes and the Angles, also from Denmark and northern Germany, established Anglo-Saxon kingdoms in Britain. The Angles gave England its name. Many "old Saxons" remained behind in Germany, forming the important historic domain of Saxony.

The Lombards invaded Italy in the sixth century and gave their name to the northern Italian region of Lombardy. The Vandals, who were especially fierce, invaded southern Gaul in the fifth century, moved on into Spain, gave their name to Spain's southernmost region of Andalusia, and even continued on into North Africa.

The Goths, who are believed to have come from Sweden, settled in the third century in an area north of the Black Sea. Some time later they split into two groups, one known as the Ostrogoths or East Goths and the other as the Visigoths or West Goths.

To further complicate the game of musical chairs that was being played by Germanic tribes all over Europe, a new barbarian people now arrived—the Huns, from Asia. Under their fearsome leader, Attila, these nomadic horsemen took up headquarters in Hungary, subjugating the Ostrogoths and exacting tribute from most of central and eastern Europe for many years. Attila was defeated in Gaul in 451, but until his death in 453 the Huns continued to control most of the land north of the Danube from the Rhine River to the Caspian Sea.

While the Ostrogoths, who had been dragged westward

by the Huns, remained settled in Hungary, the Visigoths were pushed west and south by the advancing Huns. They followed the Vandals into Spain where they subdued them and held sway until the Moorish invasions of 711. The Visigoths also invaded Italy and were among the most de-

structive of the barbarian forces that took advantage of the weakened and crumbling Roman Empire.

It was not until the early Middle Ages that the barbarian scramble for land, loot, and *Lebensraum* abated and most of Europe began to settle down to a period of relative quiet.

"Nay, they actually think it tame and stupid to acquire by the sweat of the toil what they might win by blood," Tacitus wrote of the tribes of Germany in the year 98. Although it was still early in the barbarian era, there is little reason to believe that later groups lived very differently. Tacitus, although a citizen of militaristic and imperialistic Rome, was awed by the iron authority of the Germanic tribal leaders, the fierce loyalty of the warriors, and the rigidity of the Germanic code of warfare.

In battle, he recorded, "it is a disgrace for the chief to be surpassed in valor, a disgrace for his followers not to equal the valor of the chief. . . ." Yet "feasts and entertainments, which, though inelegant, are plentifully furnished, are their only pay." To challenge an enemy and to be wounded was the highest possible honor.

Some historians see in the Germans of a later era a resemblance to their tribal ancestors in their unswerving loyalty to an imperialist kaiser or even a crazed dictator, and to a fatherland bent on world conquest. Nor is it unlikely that the dueling fraternities that still flourish in German universities are an extension of early tribal practices in Germany.

The purpose of the fraternity duel is to give both opponents an opportunity to display unflinching courage in a slashing saber fight so that they may drive out the "inner pig" of cowardice and laziness that, it is believed, lurks in each man. A secondary but very important aim is to acquire the shiny red dueling scar across cheek or forehead that is the lifelong symbol of honor and is considered a badge of membership in an elite "club."

Tacitus tells us that the warriors of the Germanic tribes spent their time in idleness, sleeping, and feasting when not fighting. The women, children, and old men did the work of the household, tended the flocks and herds, raised the grain and the few vegetables that were eaten, baked the bread, and brewed "a liquor for drinking . . . made out of barley or other grain, and fermented into a certain resemblance to wine." With reference to the latter, which was really a beer, Tacitus advises us that the Germanic men were rather intemperate and were likely to overindulge.

Mead, prepared from honey and water fermented by barley malt, was another favorite alcoholic beverage. Boar meat, horsemeat, and wild fowl hunted by the men and boys of the tribes rounded out the crude but adequate barbarian meals.

Tacitus describes the women of the Germanic tribes as being fair-haired, placid, and faithful, bearing many children and doing onerous field and household chores without complaint. Indeed, traditional German womanhood has been characterized by the words *Kinder, Küche, und Kirche* (children, kitchen, and church), an attitude that seems to have its origins in barbarian tribal life.

The church, however, had not yet come on the scene in barbarian times in Germany. The resistance to Rome also meant resistance to Christianity. Nature worship was the religion of the tribes in Germany. The warriors sang hymns to the pagan gods before going into battle. Specific trees or entire forest groves were sanctified and consecrated to deities that sprang from the forces of nature. These gods are abundant in German mythology.

It is believed that reverence for nature, especially for woodlands, has been an effective force in preserving the forests of Germany over the centuries. At any rate, scientific forestry as practiced in Germany today has a very long history.

BEER BREWING AND SAUSAGE MAKING IN THE MIDDLE AGES

After the fall of the Roman Empire the Franks emerged as the strongest of the old Germanic peoples. Under Charlemagne, who came to the throne in A.D. 768, the Frankish empire included the countries that are today France, Germany, Belgium, the Netherlands, Austria, Switzerland, northern Italy, and even the eastern part of Spain. During Charlemagne's reign the pagan Saxons and other heathen peoples in Germany accepted Christianity.

But the Frankish empire was a loose, sprawling aggregation of territories. And even when it was divided up and the eastern part fell under the rule of Charlemagne's grandson, Louis the German, there was no real political unity. Former tribal leaders engaged in ceaseless petty wars to increase their holdings and raise their rank. Some attained kingship, and the title of Holy Roman Emperor was frequently bestowed on a German ruler. Election to this exalted rank was for life, but it was little more than a title, often purchased by bribing the electors. And as historians have pointed out, the Holy Roman Empire was neither holy nor Roman, nor was it even an empire, although it survived in name until 1806.

In the early Middle Ages most of Germany lived on feudal estates patterned after the old Roman *latifundia*, large country villas surrounded by fields and meadows and worked, in Roman times, by slaves. In medieval Germany the lot of the peasants who were tied to the soil was little better than that of slaves. Trade was almost at a standstill, food was limited in choice and low in nutritional value, and deficiency diseases abounded.

One important historical development, however, was to save the German peasant from the dim and bestial future of serfdom. This was the growth of the German medieval towns.

One of the earliest of these towns was Frankfurt, which originally had been a Roman outpost situated on the Main River at a point where the river was shallow enough to be forded. Merchants and other travelers going from the Mediterranean area to northern Europe chose to cross the Main here for it was the easiest north-south river crossing in Germany. About the year 500 the Franks took over the former Roman holding and founded a settlement. It was known as the "ford of the Franks," and hence the city that grew up on that site came to be known as Frankfurt, or Frankfurt-am-Main.

One seldom thinks, while gobbling a juicy frankfurter, about the joy of finding a shallow river crossing in a harsh and rugged wilderness. But that is the origin of the word frankfurter. Frankfurt was not the only German locality to have a species of *Wurst* named after it. Besides Regensburger sausage and Thuringer sausage, there are many other such varieties best known inside Germany.

Sausage making goes back many hundreds of years before the birth of Christ. Homer mentions sausages in the *Odyssey*, written in about the ninth century B.C., and it is almost certain that some late Neolithic peoples prepared sausages by stuffing scraps of meat into natural tubular casings of pig, sheep, or ox gut.

The Romans learned sausage making from the Greeks and developed it into a high art. Marcus Apicius, the famous Roman gourmet and cookbook writer who lived from about 80 B.C. to A.D. 40, gave recipes for several kinds of sausage, and of course hot sausages and meat balls were sold in cookshops in the streets of ancient Rome.

The sausage-making skills developed by the Romans did not really begin to penetrate into Germany until the relatively stable era of the early Middle Ages. Many Germans, in fact, still refer to the frankfurter as *Wienerwurst* (Vienna sausage) because sausage making began earlier in Austria, which lay closer to Italy. This is why, in the United States, frankfurters are often called wieners.

The inhabitants of Germany, with their abundance of pork and beef, had long been a great meat-eating people. Sausage making provided a means of preserving and at the same time varying the meat consumed. It also offered an opportunity to utilize almost every part of the animal.

Thus we have in Germany today *Blutwurst* and *Milzwurst*, *Leberwurst*, *Leberkäse*, and many types of headcheese sausage. The first of these, *Blutwurst*, is blood sausage, known as "blood and tongue" when there are small pieces of tongue embedded in it. *Milzwurst* is spleen sausage. *Leberwurst* is liver sausage (the best known is Braunschweiger); *Leberkäse* is liver "cheese," a smooth paté eaten either hot or

cold; headcheese is prepared with bits of meat from the head of the hog, spiced and set in aspic. But neither of these last two has any cheese in it.

These variety-meat sausages are merely a sampling. Since the Middle Ages, Germany has been developing a variety of sausages, until there are now about three hundred different kinds. Even in a fairly small German town, the local sausage shop that does not offer several dozen different kinds of sausage at one time is considered hardly worth patronizing.

Bratwurst and *Knockwurst*, *Weisswurst* and *Bockwurst*—

to the inexperienced sausage shopper it is bewildering to choose from the sausage maker's showcase. Some sausages are ready to eat; some must first be cooked by boiling, frying, or grilling; some are smoked, some pickled; some soft, some hard.

Bratwurst ("fry" sausage) is made of fresh, coarsely ground, seasoned pork and is usually grilled. *Bratwürste*, a specialty of Nuremberg, are small and thin, similar to the link sausages popular in the United States. They are eaten by the half-dozen along with mustard and horseradish, and a dedicated German sausage eater may put away as many as two dozen as a hearty snack.

Knockwurst (or Regensburger) is familiar to most Americans as a stout frankfurter. Like the frankfurter, it is a smoked, precooked sausage prepared with beef and pork, or all beef, and seasoned with garlic. *Weisswurst* is a delicate white sausage made principally of ground veal that is mildly seasoned and lightly pickled in brine. It is the sausage traditionally eaten at the famous Munich beer festival or *Oktoberfest*.

Bock beer time in the spring brings the accompanying sausage, *Bockwurst*, to the tables of beer halls all over Germany. *Bockwurst* is similar to *Weisswurst*, although in Berlin *Bockwurst* is a smoked, reddish, frankfurter-like sausage sold at hotdog stands throughout the city.

Schinkenwurst (ham sausage) is a ready-to-eat pork sausage containing pieces of ham. In the United States it is called "ham boloney." Germany also produces many hard, salami-like sausages that keep well without refrigeration. They are called "summer sausages" and are very popular with German outdoorsmen and with family picnic groups.

If Frankfurt was the home of one of Germany's and the world's most popular sausages, this ancient city is also distinguished for having produced the literary genius Johann Wolfgang von Goethe, and Meyer Rothschild, the founder of the famous banking family, both in the 1700s. Johann Gutenberg, perhaps the first man to print from movable type, was born in the nearby city of Mainz, and books were already being printed in Frankfurt in the 1400s.

Another German city that traces its history to the early Middle Ages is Munich, which in the 700s was referred to as *zu den Mönchen* (at the monks') because it was the site of a famous monastery. Later it came to be known, in German, as *München*; in English, Munich.

During the early Middle Ages, the monasteries were the truck gardens and beer breweries, confectioneries and bakeries of Europe, as well as the craft centers and workshops, hospitals, and travelers' havens. Towns were few, roads were danger-fraught, and the nobles who owned the feudal estates were more interested in warfare than welfare.

Charlemagne, aware of these aspects of medieval life, asked the monasteries of his empire to grow certain herbs, seeds, and other plants, particularly parsley, dill, and caraway, and to brew beer. Parsley and dill have since been extensively used in central European cooking, and caraway seed, which had been produced by the Swiss lake dwellers, came into even wider use. As to the directive to brew beer, the monastery at Munich must have responded with exceptional enthusiasm for this city is today one of the principal beer-brewing centers of the world.

Of the many kinds of beer brewed in ancient and medieval times, the type developed at Munich became the standard for types drunk in the Western world today. It was in Munich that the first *Brauhaus*, the brewery-operated beer hall restaurant, was opened. With *Brauhausen*, the rule seems to be the bigger the better. There are Munich beer halls capable of seating thousands of people. From mid-morning to well past midnight, the beer hall invites serious or casual beer drinking, with or without sausages or other hearty food. The atmosphere is informal, often reminiscent of the joviality of the Middle Ages, with shared tables, much merriment, possibly a brass band and a garden for use in summer.

Prosit is the Latin-based word that the Germans have adopted for their national toast. Its exact meaning is "may it profit you" or "may it do [you] good," but of course its implication is "to your health," and it is heard everywhere and often in Germany's beer halls.

Germans have always preferred their beer served in a ceramic stein with a handle rather than in a glass or metal mug. The stein helps keep the beer at the moderately cool temperature that most Germans like, not warm but not too chilled. What goes into the stein is even more important. One never asks for just beer. One specifies the brew and the quantity; one asks for *helles* (light) or *dunkles* (dark).

One may ask for bock beer, the sweet, heavy dark beer brewed in the fall that appears the following spring. Or one may prefer *Weissbier* (white beer), which is brewed from wheat and is sometimes served *mit Schuss*, a splash of raspberry concentrate to counteract the somewhat tart flavor. In Germany, one can even have egg in his beer simply by asking for *Heisses Eierbier*, a hot beer punch, sweetened, enriched with milk and eggs, and beaten to a froth.

Munich received an early start as a major German city from its favorable location in Bavaria, south of the Danube on the Isar River. Frankfurt too was favored by circumstances of location. Other medieval German cities had to develop the hard way. Often a town was the outgrowth of a local market established just outside the castle walls of a nobleman's fortified holding. As trade increased and the market folk became more prosperous, they might combine their resources to buy a charter for a free town from the feudal lord who had overextended himself through petty wars or high living.

From the thirteenth to the sixteenth centuries, such towns began to spring up all over Germany. Gradually the peasants discovered that they did not have to remain bound to the soil in order to get enough to eat. The complex life of the towns offered a variety of ways of earning a living. It was true of course that, as in medieval towns all over Europe, living conditions were congested and unsanitary. The streets ran with filth, many habitations were ramshackle and unsafe, and fire and pestilence were commonplace.

But the towns offered opportunity; the fixed life of feudal estates did not. Soon an independent and prosperous merchant and artisan class arose. Wealth brought better dwellings, stately town halls, and handsome, spired churches. Today in many German cities there is an old quarter that dates from the Middle Ages and has retained its narrow, cobbled lanes and tall, steep-gabled houses with their half-timbered façades, all looking very much like an illustration from Grimm's fairy tales.

At Augsburg in southern Germany, not very far from Munich, one can visit the *Fuggerei*, a group of sturdy and

picturesque medieval houses built in the sixteenth century and still occupied. Erected by Jacob Fugger of the famous merchant and banking family, these fifty-two dwellings were built as a workers' housing project and let at minimal rents. This was probably the first such social settlement anywhere.

The Fuggers, whose fortune originated in the textile trade, rose to prominence in the fifteenth and sixteenth centuries, diversifying their enterprises and extending their wealth and influence throughout Europe. Augsburg was one of the German free cities during the Middle Ages, and like many other such cities it displayed the architectural glories and enjoyed the rich cultural life of a small, prosperous kingdom.

Evidence of the culturally advanced life of many medieval German towns can be seen in the institution of the Master-singers. These were groups of local craftsmen and businessmen who banded together to form music guilds. In their leisure hours they composed music with accompanying verses, a hobby which they took very seriously.

Their periodic songfests, which were really prize contests for beauty and originality of composition, were events of great importance. The songs rendered by the contestants were rated according to very strict rules, and the societies themselves were set up, like other medieval guilds, with rigid membership categories. One progressed through the ranks from "pupil" to "friend" to "singer" to "poet," and finally to "master" on the basis of skill.

The inspiration for the Mastersingers, who flourished in cities like Nuremberg and Mainz between the 1300s and the 1500s, came from the Minnesingers of an earlier day. *Minne* is the Old German word for love. The Minnesingers were

wandering minstrels, usually of noble blood, who entertained at German feudal castles in the 1100s and 1200s. They too wrote their own music and verses and sang principally of love and of the traditions of knighthood.

Richard Wagner's opera *Die Meistersinger von Nürnberg* offers a delightful glimpse of sixteenth-century German town life as well as a portrait of a famous real-life Master-singer, the shoemaker Hans Sachs.

As the medieval towns prospered, those that were located on the North Sea or on navigable rivers began to develop a sea trade. During the thirteenth and fourteenth centuries, some of these cities began to band together to protect their common mercantile interests. Their organization came to be known as the Hanseatic League and their ships soon controlled the fur trade with Russia, the wool trade with Flanders, and the fish trade with Scandinavia. Bremen, Lübeck, and Hamburg, all in northern Germany, became the principal Hanseatic cities.

The Hansa sea trade opened new sources of wealth to medieval Germany. It also brought several exotic foods to German cities, foods that would have taken much longer to reach central Europe had they traveled by the land routes of the Middle Ages. One of these foods was sauerkraut from, of all places, China.

No one knows exactly when sauerkraut originated, but it is older than the Great Wall of China, much of which was built in the third century B.C. The 1500-mile-long wall took hundreds of years to complete, and the workers who put it together brick by brick and stone by stone lived principally on cabbage and rice wine. In winter the cabbage was cut up and soured in the rice wine to preserve it.

It was this soured cabbage that the marauding Tartars of Mongolia (against whom the wall had been built) brought westward with them when they invaded Russia and Poland in the thirteenth century. The Tartars had by then devised their own method of salting and preserving cabbage. The Russians soon adopted it from them, and the Hansa sea traders in turn brought it back to Germany from Russia, an extra dividend from their profitable fur traffic.

Sauerkraut has since become indispensable to the German menu. It can be eaten raw, but in Germany it is more often cooked and served hot, flavored with caraway or onion, apple, or juniper berries. Frequently the kraut is sautéed in lard or poultry fat at the start of the cooking to add flavor.

Eating sausages and cooked pork dishes such as roasts, chops, spareribs and pigs' knuckles without sauerkraut is unthinkable. A Berlin specialty is *Eisbein mit Sauerkraut* (pork hocks with sauerkraut) served with another Berlin specialty, *Erbsenpüree*, a purée of cooked yellow split-peas thickened with flour, flavored with sautéed onion, and often baked to produce a crusty brown topping. A popular combination plate throughout Germany is the *Schlactplatte* (butcher's platter) composed of a variety of sausages and smoked cooked meats and, of course, sauerkraut.

Even before sauerkraut came ashore in Germany it had been added to ship's stores for use in seagoing menus, on both German and other vessels. Long-keeping, juicy, and refreshingly tangy, it was the perfect addition to the seaman's dreary and limited diet. It was also extremely healthful, as it supplied vitamin C as well as other nutrients that were usually lacking in the diet on long sea voyages.

Alexandre Dumas, writing about sauerkraut in the late nineteenth century, apparently did not share the enthusiasm of the people of northern and eastern Europe for this dish. "The Germans," he acknowledged, "are mad about it. It has become proverbial that a sure way to get oneself murdered in Italy is to say the women are not pretty; in England to tease the inhabitants about the degree of liberty they enjoy; in Germany to question whether sauerkraut is a dish for the gods."

The Hamburg sea merchants of the Hanseatic League brought another new food back to Germany from Russia and the Baltic lands, one that had especially far-reaching possibilities. It was a dish of raw beef chopped into small particles and molded into a kind of patty or small, flat cake. The meat was served with various condiments so that each person could flavor it to his liking. In Germany these side dishes soon included raw egg yolk, capers, gherkins, finely chopped onion, anchovy filets, and of course salt and pepper. The dish was called after the same Tartar hordes who had brought sauerkraut to the West. It became known as steak Tartar, or beef Tartar.

The Tartar horseman impatiently scraping away at a chunk of raw meat on the Asian steppes could not have realized that his hasty meal would one day be an elegant and costly dish. For the beef for steak Tartar must be of excellent quality and it should not be ground but rather *scraped*, so that only the most tender particles of meat are collected. In Germany, steak Tartar is sometimes served as a main course, but more often it appears as an appetizer to an elaborate dinner.

It was inevitable that someone would one day decide to cook one of the raw Hamburg beef patties, broiling or frying it like sausage, and perhaps adding some filler and flavoring to the meat before cooking. Hamburg steak, or *Deutsches "beefsteak"* as it is called in Hamburg nowadays, is a thick, oval patty, grilled or pan-broiled and usually served with fried sweet onions. And there is no end to the meat loaves, meat balls, stuffings, dumplings and other chopped-meat dishes, or to the variety of ingredients added to the meat for flavoring, bulk, and texture.

Germany's most popular meat balls, really meat dumplings, are *Königsberger Klopse*, named for the former East Prussian capital of Königsberg, once a Hanseatic city. The ground meat is mixed with eggs, stale rolls that have been soaked in water, onions, and anchovies. It is then shaped into plum-sized balls and cooked in boiling beef stock. The *Klopse* are served in a caper-strewn sauce made from the thickened stock.

Königsberger Klopse are a far-out version of the hamburger as it is known in the United States. A chef at the St. Louis World's Fair of 1904 is supposed to have introduced Americans to the grilled meat patty served on a bun, which almost at once took on the name of hamburger. German immigrants were numerous in the Midwest at the time and for a long time they had been preparing Hamburg's chopped-meat dishes in their kitchens.

Ten years later, when World War I broke out and everything German became suspect in America, hamburgers went by the name of Salisbury steak for a while. The name was derived from Dr. James Salisbury, a nineteenth-century British nutritionist who had made rather extravagant claims for the healing and nourishing effects of a diet composed of ground beef and tea.

Sauerkraut, steak Tartar, and hamburger were not the only contributions of the Hanseatic cities of medieval Germany. The sea trade extended to southern Europe, Africa, and the East as well as to Baltic and North Sea waters. From distant ports the merchant ships brought many of the herbs and spices used to season German cookery. Among these were the capers, really pickled flower buds, used in shellfish dishes and in bland meat dishes; the mustard seed and accompanying seasonings that give German mustards their hot, zesty flavor; the anise, ginger, and cardamom that contribute such mouth-watering appeal to German baked goods and especially to German Christmas cookies.

GERMAN UNIFICATION AND GERMAN REGIONAL COOKERY

Germany was still a long way from unification in the closing centuries of the Middle Ages. No single German state was strong enough to dominate the others. The small kingdoms, duchies, and independent cities seemed destined to thrive contentedly as fragments of some larger but vague entity.

Few German rulers took much notice when in 1415 the old German Hohenzollern dynasty gained control of the large eastern district of Brandenburg and began to increase its holdings in Prussia. However, by 1701 Prussia was powerful enough to be declared a kingdom under the Hohenzollern monarch, Frederick I. Its strong, rigidly disciplined army was directed by generals from the wealthy aristocratic landowning class of Prussia, the Junkers.

Frederick II (Frederick the Great) came to the Prussian throne in 1740. He further increased Prussia's territory at the expense of Poland and Austria, expounded the theory of government that "might makes right," and accordingly made Prussia the foremost military power in Europe.

Prussian might was felt inside the kingdom as well. When food shortages threatened the towns and cities of Prussia in the 1700s, Frederick II did not merely suggest that the farmers plant potatoes (which had been introduced to Europe from the New World two centuries earlier). He *ordered* that potatoes be planted, and threatened disobedient farmers with the death penalty. Prussians began to plant potatoes with a vengeance.

As a consequence Germany became one of the world's leading potato-eating nations. The average German today eats 680 pounds of potatoes a year, nearly two pounds a day. This means that potatoes appear on the German dinner table daily, most often as *Salzkartoffeln* ("salt" potatoes). They are boiled in salted water, drained and steamed very dry, then dressed with melted butter and such flavor-makers as parsley, dill, minced onion, caraway seed, bread crumbs, or bits of ham or bacon.

The German answer to French fries is *Bratkartoffeln*, German fried potatoes. These are thin-sliced potatoes, fried brown and tender in shallow lard or bacon fat, usually with some diced onion. And what could be more German than *Kartoffelpuffer*, potato pancakes, prepared with grated and seasoned raw potato and served with mixed stewed fruit or applesauce, alone or as a meat accompaniment?

The Germans carry their liking for the fruit-and-potato combination a step further in a popular dish called *Himmel und Erde* (heaven and earth) which blends seasoned mashed potato and warm applesauce. This dish is a specialty of the Rhineland.

Kartoffelsalat, potato salad, either the cold type or the hot variety tossed with crumbled bacon and a vinegary onion-and-bacon-fat dressing, is another German specialty. *Kartoffelklösse*, potato dumplings, are prepared in various ways using either cooked or raw potatoes, or a combination of the two. In any case, they are solid, rib-sticking fare.

Potato starch often serves as a sauce thickener in Germany in lieu of cornstarch. And potatoes are found in soups, stews, and even—cooked and smoothly mashed—as an ingredient in chocolate cake.

Otto von Bismarck, who became prime minister of Prussia in 1862, declared early in his career that the problems of the future would be solved not by speeches and resolutions, but by "blood and iron." By 1871, after fighting wars with Denmark, Austria, and France, Bismarck had brought about the long-sought unification, and King Wilhelm I of Prussia became the emperor of Germany.

But unification could not erase the regionalisms that were rooted in the German topography and had become rooted to some extent, too, in the German spirit. Particularly bitter toward the Prussians were the south Germans, who resented doing military service in the Prussian-dominated army.

Religion had also been a divisive factor in Germany since the sixteenth century, when Martin Luther's protests against many of the practices of the Roman Catholic Church started the Reformation. By and large northern and central Germany turned Protestant while most of southern Germany, the Rhineland in the west, and the Polish-speaking population of eastern Prussia kept the Roman Catholic faith.

Another north-south difference was, and still is, that of language. A variety of dialects exists throughout Germany, but especially marked is the *Plattdeutsch* or Low German spoken in the northern part of the country. With its low-lying sandy coastal flats, its windmills, dykes, and canals, northern Germany, on both its North Sea and Baltic Sea coasts, resembles Holland. So, too, the "flat" dialect of the north country resembles Dutch and is more closely related to English than the German spoken farther south.

Plattdeutsch lost its status as a written language in the sixteenth century and books and newspapers throughout Germany today are printed in *Hochdeutsch* or High German, the spoken dialect of the central and southern regions. But it should be pointed out that "low" and "high" as applied

to the German language do not refer to the social, intellectual, or economic status of the people; they apply simply to the elevation of the land.

Traveling southward from the coastal beaches and the green heaths of the bordering inland plains, one approaches increasingly rolling country. The Harz Mountains, noted for the fine singing canaries raised in that vicinity, boast the highest peak in central Germany, the Brocken. Over 3,700 feet high, it is said to be the mist-shrouded site of witches' revels, particularly on Walpurgis Night, April 30. Today the Brocken lies just inside the border of East Germany.

Southern Germany is the most mountainous region, with the Black Forest in its western corner and the 9,721-foot *Zugspitze* in Bavaria, on the border with Austria. Garmisch-Partenkirschen, the famed summer resort and winter sports center, nestles in the valley below, surrounded by abrupt Alpine peaks. Oberammergau, scene of the awesome Passion Play which portrays the suffering and death of Jesus, is nearby. Ordinarily the Passion Play is given every ten years and requires 1,250 performers. The Passion Play was first performed in 1634 in fulfillment of a vow to present it every decade if the Black Plague were lifted from the land.

Also in the Bavarian Alps is the winter resort village of Berchtesgaden. On a nearby mountain peak Adolf Hitler maintained his mountain retreat, the "Eagle's Nest" where he plotted some of his most brutal campaigns of conquest and annihilation.

The dialects of the south German regions of Baden and Bavaria employ a great many colorful expressions that are

not found in the more northerly dialects. Like the Austrians, the south Germans are fond of whimsy, are imaginative, and often add diminutive endings to their words. Thus a *Wurst* becomes a *Würstl*, a "little sausage," although it may not necessarily be smaller than any other sausage; a potato is no longer a *Kartoffel* but an *Erdäpfel*, an "earth apple."

There are marked differences between northern and southern styles of German architecture. The south has the same Italian-influenced baroque buildings that one finds in Austria. Fanciful onion-shaped church steeples contrast sharply with the austere pointed steeples of the north. Often decorated with gift and curlicues, public buildings and palaces alike in the south are gay and gracious. In the north, ornamentation seems to have been scrubbed away by the Reformation; severity of line is often encountered, and brick is used extensively in building since neither stone nor wood was ever as plentiful on the coastal plain as farther south.

Southern Germany is generously endowed with clear mountain lakes set against a backdrop of evergreen forests and snowy peaks. The Rhine, Germany's most important river, rises in Switzerland and flows 700 miles through Germany and Holland where it empties through a broad delta into the North Sea. Although the Rhine only flows 443 miles past German soil, Germany's history and legends as well as her commercial and industrial wealth are bound up with it.

In German mythology, the famous ring of the Nibelungen dwarfs was forged from gold hoarded deep in the waters of the Rhine and guarded by the Rhine maidens. The Nibelungen ring was said to confer power over the entire world upon its possessor. Richard Wagner's four great "Ring" operas tell the story of the forging of the ring, its loss, the struggle for its repossession, and its eventual return to the waters of the Rhine where, for all we know, it reposes to this day.

The Rhine valley of southern Germany is a picturesque land of castles and vineyards. But as the river flows northward toward the centers of heavy industry such as Cologne and Düsseldorf and the coal-mining region of the Ruhr, its waters become polluted with chemical refuse, its atmosphere

turns hazy with smoke, and its scenery gives offense rather than pleasure to the eye. This is the price West Germany pays for its leadership in the manufacture of steel, chemicals, plastics, dyes, textiles, paper, and many other important products.

More pastoral is the eastward course of the Danube through southern Germany. It flows principally through neat rural villages and old medieval towns, sturdy and attractive, their factories inconspicuous. It is to the village of Donaueschingen in the Black Forest that tourists go to visit the *Donauquelle*, or Danube Spring. Here a masonry-enclosed pool catches a mountain stream claimed to be the true source of the Danube. Statuary alongside the pool depicts a mother pointing out to the infant Danube the easterly path it must take toward the Black Sea.

Actually there are three streams, the two small rivers Brigach and Breg and the smaller stream of the *Donauquelle*, that come together at Donaueschingen to take the name

Danube. The Brigach is perhaps a truer source of the Danube, for its tiny underground spring trickling into a mossy pool in one of the farming valleys of the Black Forest actually precedes the other two streams. But the burghers of Donaueschingen would no doubt give claimants from Brigach a difficult time should they give voice to such an opinion.

Climate also is a variable in Germany. In the mountains of the south the higher elevations receive quite a lot of snow and rather cold weather. But cities nearer sea level, such as Frankfurt, are relatively warm and sheltered. Northwestern Germany also has a temperate climate, for it receives the warming influence of the North Atlantic Drift, a continuation of the Gulf Stream.

Germany's Baltic region in the northeast, however, is cut off from this tempering influence by Schleswig-Holstein and Denmark which form a stem of land that juts northward. Thus northeast Germany, which is really a continuation of the great plain of northern Asia, suffers extremes of temperature. Summers are very hot and winters bring icy winds from Russia. But in general Germany's climate is not nearly so severe as one might expect in terms of her latitude. Shifted to the same latitude in North America, Germany would be as chilly as that part of Canada that lies between the Great Lakes and Hudson Bay.

Regional differences show up in Germany's cuisine as well as in her climate, terrain, religion, architecture, language, and temperament. In northern Germany—especially in Schleswig-Holstein, which borders on and was once a part of Denmark—dairy products and fish maintain an important place in the cuisine. Seafood dishes are often smothered in an egg- and cream-rich sauce, and boiled or poached fish may be dressed with horseradish-flavored whipped cream.

Herring, a favorite meal starter now popular everywhere in Germany, originated in the north. There are many varieties: the young reddish-pink herring called *Matjes*; the fat white herring known as *Schmaltz*; Bismarck herring; and the sharp everyday salt herring.

A small glass or two of *Schnaps*, a fiery colorless distilled liquor, is often tossed down with the thirst-inducing herring at the start of a meal. *Schnaps* is sometimes referred to as *Korn* after the ancient word for grain, from which it is distilled. Followed by beer, *Korn* provides a potent boilermaker. Germany's northern neighbors down similar alcoholic mixtures, no doubt as a bracer against the climate: aquavit with a beer chaser for the Scandinavians, gin followed by beer for the Dutch, Scotch and beer for the Scots.

Fish-and-meat combinations are typical of northern Germany, as seen in the use of anchovies with veal in *Holsteiner Schnitzel*, and in the popular sailor's hash called *Labskaus*. This dish dates back to the early Hanseatic era when there was no refrigeration and ships had to put in stores of pickled or otherwise preserved, long-keeping foods. *Labskaus* combines pickled pork or corned beef, boiled potatoes, pickled beets or dill pickles, herring, and sometimes anchovies as well. It is a specialty of the German port city of Hamburg, although one would suppose that sailors had had enough of it at sea. Servings of *Labskaus* are usually topped with a fried egg, just as is *Holsteiner Schnitzel*.

Hamburg has other specialties typical of the northern coast. Restaurants called *Austernstuben* serve oysters accompanied by red wine and sharply flavored cheese. Hamburgers enjoy *Aalsuppe* (eel soup) with its roster of such unlikely ingredients as prunes, white wine, vinegar, and green peas combined with chunks of fresh eel.

Also well liked in Hamburg are fruit soups made with cherries, apples, plums, or berries. These soups are popular too in nearby Scandinavia and in eastern Europe. Winy and cinnamony, German fruit soups are often served cold, topped with a puff of whipped cream or a spoonful of sour cream, or with cooked dumplings of sugar-and-egg-white meringue.

Fruit soups served either hot or cold, in summer or in winter, are refreshing and appealing. But with his usual disparagement of things German, Alexandre Dumas in his *Great Dictionary of Cuisine* says of German cherry soup (known as *Kirschkaltschale*): "It is only for the record that we mention this execrable dish of crushed cherries and ground-up pits, ferociously spiced, drowned in wine, and served cold." Dumas' reference to "ground-up pits" derives from the German practice of adding a few coarsely pounded cherry pits to the soup to intensify the flavor.

Hamburg is Germany's second largest city and lies on the Elbe River about fifty-five miles inland from the North Sea. Much of the city is built on piles and it is crisscrossed by canals. A great port, Hamburg is international in spirit and also very much a sailor's town. Its St. Pauli quarter is famous, even notorious, for its lively night life.

The cuisines of the Rhineland, in western Germany, and of the region just south of it bordering on Alsace-Lorraine show marked French influence. The long-disputed, now French, provinces of Alsace and Lorraine have been shunted back and forth between France and Germany since the days of Charlemagne. Almost every time Germany grew fat, it meant that she had once again gobbled up this desirable chunk of territory on her border with France.

Western Germany is a wine-growing region, particularly in the valleys of the Rhine and the Moselle rivers. Most German table wines are light, fruity white wines. Although some reds are produced they are not generally so distinguished as the white wines. Wine requires more delicately flavored food than does beer and consequently there are fewer vinegary, salty, and sweet-and-sour dishes in Rhineland cookery. Sausages and rolls, however, are considered very good company for wine—and in the Rhineland this trio is known as *Weck, Wurst, und Wein* (roll, sausage, and wine).

A specialty of Frankfurt in west central Germany is *Apfelwein* (apple wine). This beverage, which tastes something like white grape wine, may be obtained in Frankfurt taverns designated as apple-wine inns. A traditional accompaniment to *Apfelwein* is the delightfully named dish *Käse mit Musik* (cheese with music). For this dish, slices of semi-soft German cheese, usually *Handkäse* (hand cheese), are topped with vinegar, oil, and finely chopped onion and eaten on pumpernickel or rye bread.

The apple-wine inns of Frankfurt are noisy and informal, very much like the beer halls of Munich. Often there is

accordion music, and strangers at common tables join together in singing.

The cooking of southern Germany, especially Bavaria, is what most people think of as being typically German. Munich, almost at the heart of this region, stands for beer brewing and sausage making. This is also the Germany of pork and dumplings, red cabbage, and sauerkraut.

Dumplings are a culinary species unto themselves. In Germany they may appear at any point in the meal. Liver or meat dumplings go into beef, veal, or chicken broth; flour, bread, or potato dumplings accompany gravy-rich meat dishes; sweet dumplings filled with fruit or prepared with cottage cheese turn up for dessert.

Most dumpling mixtures begin with a starch such as flour, farina, or bread crumbs to which egg and either water or milk are added. Dumplings may be as tiny as almonds or as large as oranges (or even larger). They are boiled in water or broth, and are sometimes then browned by frying or baking. Dumplings are seldom feathery, and they add considerable caloric value to an already rich diet. The German menu, which is not as meat-poor as that of southern Europe, for example, could probably do without them, but the German dumpling lover evidently cannot.

Maultaschen, ravioli-like dough pockets stuffed with a meat-and-spinach mixture, are a great favorite in Swabia, the region of south central Germany that lies just to the west of Bavaria. *Maultaschen* may be served in soup or simply drained and eaten with melted butter or with a sauce. Another Swabian specialty is *Spätzle*, small, firm-dough flour dumplings. These may also be served in soup or as a side dish.

Although Germany has limited access to the sea, she consumes a wide variety and a substantial quantity of fish: herring, cod, and shellfish from the North and Baltic seas; salmon from the Rhine; pike from the Moselle; sheatfish from the Danube; and carp from fresh-water ponds everywhere. In southern Germany, *Forelle* (trout) from the mountain streams of the Black Forest is a highly prized dish, particularly when it is prepared in the style known as *blaugekocht* (blue-cooked). In order to be cooked "blue" the trout must be extremely fresh, for the color is produced through the application of vinegar to the skin. The vinegar acts upon a substance in the fish's skin that evaporates very soon after the fish has died.

Another blue dish is *Blaukraut* (blue cabbage). Actually this is red cabbage (*Rotkohl*) which turns a deep purple in the cooking. A favorite way to prepare red cabbage in southern Germany is to braise it with apples, onion, and diced bacon.

Desserts in southern Germany tend to be richer and more elaborate than in the north. *Bayrische Creme* (Bavarian cream), a molded pudding of eggs, cream, and gelatin, may be flavored with vanilla, or with chocolate, wine, rum, coffee, lemon, or other fruits. *Schwarzwälder Kirschtorte* is the famed Black Forest cherry torte, an overwhelmingly rich cake of chocolate layers, chocolate cream filling, sweet cherries, Kirsch-flavored whipped cream, and shaved chocolate. *Kirsch* or *Kirschwasser*, a potent liquor distilled from the fermented juice of cherries, has been produced in the Black Forest region for centuries.

The region of eastern Germany lies largely within the separate country of East Germany and its cuisine is closely related to that of eastern Europe. The influence of Czecho-slovakian cookery, with its mammoth dumplings and its use of caraway, mushrooms, and sour cream, can be seen here. Pork and sauerkraut dishes are common in this region; goose is well liked, as it is throughout eastern Europe; carp is a favorite fish, often prepared sweet-and-sour in the Polish and Bohemian fashion, with vinegar, sugar, spices, and raisins. Dried peas, beans, and lentils, along with potatoes, provide a basic low-cost starch diet in this least prosperous region of Germany.

In Berlin the great specialty is *Gelbe Erbsensuppe*, yellow split-pea soup, thick and rib-sticking against the often bone-chilling winds of the northeast. It is served in countless quick-lunch establishments and may be had plain or with slices of *Bockwurst* or with dumplings in it.

Berlin of course lies in East Germany, 110 miles from the West German border. Once the capital of Prussia and later the capital of Germany, this city is now itself divided. It is a symbol of the larger division, that of the two Ger-manies. East Berlin serves as the capital of East Germany. The capital of West Germany has been removed to Bonn on the Rhine.

East Germany was the Soviet sector following World War II and it is still Communist-governed. Its hard-working people enjoy few luxuries, for this part of Germany is largely agricultural, relatively poor in natural resources, and has not of course received the tremendous outpouring of United States aid that West Germany has.

Poverty, unrepaired war damage, and party propaganda slogans are found everywhere in East Germany. In East Berlin the once stately tree-lined avenue of Unter den Lin-den, with its famous hotels, great stores, and foreign em-bassies, is but a haunting memory of its former self. It is not surprising that East Germany, although only a little less than half the size of West Germany, has less than one third

the number of people. Many escaped to the West, especially prior to the building of the Berlin Wall in 1961.

West Berlin stands like a brightly lighted, well-peopled, and prosperous island in a gray sea. Its Kurfürstendamm, more than ever the great shopping street, is lined with gleaming new office buildings and sleek cafés, some of them with heated, glass-enclosed terraces for use in winter. As throughout West Germany, the war rubble has been cleared away, most of it piled up into artificial hills, covered with soil, and planted with grass and flowers.

Berlin's famous park, the Tiergarten, has been largely restored to its former beauty. The Battle of Berlin was fought in and around this park, causing great devastation. And in the terrible winter of 1945–46 following Germany's defeat, the trees of the Tiergarten were cut down for fuel, and potatoes were planted in what had been rose gardens.

The contrast between the two halves of Berlin is strongly

marked. One gets the impression that West Berlin is trying to forget the war; East Berlin wants to remember.

It is ironic that seventy-five years after unification, Germany should have once again been divided. It is divided today by much stronger political and economic differences than ever before existed in German history.

It is ironic, too, that Bismarck's proud state of Prussia, officially dissolved at the end of World War II, now lies scattered and unrecognizable among the countries of Poland, Russia, and East Germany. Perhaps, after all, "blood and iron" have turned out to be a less successful course of diplomacy than speeches and resolutions might have been.

Judging from the day-long procession of snacktimes and mealtimes in Germany, German appetites never even approach the point of satiation.

The day begins with *Frühstück* (breakfast). Not as skimpy as the roll-and-coffee or roll-and-chocolate repast of France and of Mediterranean Europe, the basic German breakfast usually includes soft-boiled eggs, fresh crisp rolls or thick hearty slices of bread with butter, and coffee with milk.

But by 10:30 or 11 a faint sensation of gnawing in the stomach is felt from Hamburg to Munich. It is *Brotzeit* ("bread time"), the hour for a second breakfast that often turns out to be a midmorning meal. Office workers dive into their briefcases and come up with thick sandwiches stuffed with *Wurst*, ham, or cheese.

Others forsake their work at midmorning to go in search of *Brotzeit* nourishment—beer with sausage at a Munich beer hall, or the cheese sandwich on a round roll that in Cologne is winkingly referred to as a "half chicken." The *Bäckerei* offers irresistible aromas of fresh rolls, cake, or pastry hot from the oven, served at tables along with coffee. The *Mölkerei* (dairy shop) provides a glass of milk and a choice of cheeses with bread.

SIX MEALS A DAY IN MODERN GERMANY

Cafés and informal restaurants bring forth *Belegtes Butterbrot*, open sandwiches of buttered bread topped with a choice of cold meats, fish, salads, or cheeses. Somehow, one is sustained until lunchtime.

Lunch, at noon or 1 P.M., is the big meal of the day in villages and small towns where people are likely to go home for lunch. Otherwise a "light" meal of thick soup followed by a rich dessert suffices.

Regardless of the amount consumed at lunchtime, coffeetime rolls around at 4 or 5 P.M. For those who do not go to the *Konditorei* (pastry shop) for coffee with pastry or sandwiches and for the perusal of newspapers and magazines, there are the *Wurst* stands for beer and frankfurters, or other kinds of sausages.

Dinner, between 6 and 7:30, is the big meal of the day for those who have partaken only moderately of the four previous meals. A full-course German dinner begins with *Vorspeisen* or "before-foods" such as herring or smoked eel, whitefish, or trout. Or it may begin with shellfish such as shrimp or oysters, or with lobster from Germany's Helgoland Island in the North Sea. Beef Tartar, stuffed eggs, *Wurst*, or thin-sliced Westphalian ham served with dark, thin-sliced Westphalian pumpernickel are all well-liked German dinner appetizers. A very popular *Vorspeise* salad is *Ochsenmaulsalat*. As the name implies, the main ingredient must come from the tongue or cheek of an ox, and so this salad is usually prepared with cooked slivered beef tongue in a tart, zesty dressing.

Less formal dinners may omit the *Vorspeisen*, but what German dinner will omit the soup? Soup is eaten in Germany not only at dinner but at *Brotzeit*, lunchtime, midnight, and between times as well. There is a soup to suit every whim and appetite: goulash soup, thick with meat and potatoes, adapted from the Hungarians by way of the Austrians; bean, pea, or lentil soup to combat a chill or a pang of sudden hunger; beer, wine, or fruit soup to satisfy a fancy for something tantalizing and refreshing.

At a dinner made up of several courses, however, a clear soup is usually served—a *Fleischbrühe* (meat broth) of beef or veal, or a chicken broth, afloat with noodles, dumplings, strips of pancake, or cubes of firm egg custard called *Eierstich*. *Eierstich* may also appear cut in strips, diamonds, or fancy shapes such as stars.

Most traditional German meat dishes are based on pork, beef, veal, and game. Lamb and mutton are little used in German cuisine, but variety meats ranging from brains and kidneys, hearts and sweetbreads, to things like calves' lung stew and baked udder are likely to turn up.

In the history of Germany, there has never been a lack of wood for cooking fuel. Therefore many kinds of slow-cooked meats—boiled, braised, and pot-roasted—have achieved a permanent place on the German dinner table. Among beef dishes, boiled beef with horseradish sauce and *Sauerbraten* (sweet-and-sour marinated pot roast) are perhaps the most popular.

The ancient Romans preserved haunches of cooked meat in a mixture of salt and vinegar flavored with mustard and honey. Raw meat could also be kept from spoilage by this method and, as added benefits, the meat was both tenderized and imbued with flavor during the marinating process. *Sauerbraten* is prepared in this manner, being immersed in a spicy wine or vinegar marinade for several days before cooking. There are many regional recipes for *Sauerbraten*. Some recipes give a sharp tangy *Sauerbraten*, others produce a richer and more mellow-tasting dish. Raisins and crushed *Lebkuchen* or gingersnaps are very often added to the *Sauerbraten* gravy.

In preparing *Hasenpfeffer*, probably the best-known German game dish, the hare is first marinated in vinegar, wine, onion, and spices, and is then stewed in the marinade. This process is called jugging, and so *Hasenpfeffer* translates as jugged hare. Sour cream is sometimes added at the end of the cooking to mellow the flavor. Today *Hasenpfeffer* is frequently prepared with domesticated rabbit and cannot be classified as a game dish.

But the preference for game and game birds such as pheasant, partridge, and grouse persists in Germany. Marinating game in a spiced vinegar mixture and cooking it in the marinade along with red wine, juniper berries, and spices is a very old practice in Germany whether the meat is venison, bear, hare, or wild boar. These sharply flavored mixtures are helpful in counteracting the strong, gamy flavor of most wild-animal flesh.

Tart fruits such as currants and *Preiselbeeren* (small, cranberry-like fruits) are almost always served with game in Germany. Pork dishes too seem to call for some kind of fruit accompaniment or combination. Thus *Schweinerippchen* (pork chops) are stuffed (*gefüllte*) with a raisin and apple filling, and the Hamburg specialty of *Bohnen, Birnen, und Speck* combines dried beans, pears, and bacon all cooked together. Goose is frequently stuffed with apples, prunes, and chestnuts.

Both goose and duck appear on German dinner tables on festive occasions. Chicken, which in the past had been outranked by these two, is now growing in popularity in Germany. Especially well liked are the plump little spit-roasted birds cooked rotisserie fashion and sold in city shops for a take-home dinner.

German vegetables remain largely in the cabbage, potato, and root vegetable orbit. This means plenty of kale, kohlrabi, and Brussels sprouts; carrots, beets, turnips, and parsnips; as well as red and green cabbage, and of course sauerkraut. When vegetables such as asparagus and spinach do come to market, however, they are served smothered in a creamy sauce or whipped into a rich soufflé. In southern Germany, where beer brewing is widespread and quantities of hops are grown for beer flavoring, hop shoots are cooked and eaten as a vegetable with melted butter. They have a mildly bitter flavor.

Germans like their salads sharp and vinegary rather than oily. Favorites are pickled beets, or lettuce wilted in a hot bacon-fat dressing cut with plenty of vinegar and seasoned with salt, sugar, and pepper.

While the *Konditoreien* and bakeries of Germany produce an assortment of cakes from *Schnecken* (cinnamon-filled "snails"), *Krapfen* (crullers), and *Streuselkuchen* (crumbcake) to glamorous meringue-and-nut *Torten*, baked goods are usually consumed with coffee at odd hours rather than as dessert after dinner.

Puddings prepared with milk or fruit juice and thickened with starch are often served at the close of a meal. *Rote Grütze*, a red fruit pudding of thickened cherry, raspberry, or red currant juice, or a molded purée of these fruits, is one of the most common desserts in Germany.

Very well liked also is a dessert called *Mohr im Hemd* ("Moor in a shirt"), which can be dressed up or down depending on the resources at hand. A prosperous *Mohr im Hemd* might appear as a chocolate pudding garbed in a billowing mantle of whipped cream. A more modest *Mohr* would consist of black-bread crumbs tossed with cinnamon and sugar, and clad in a vanilla sauce.

Heartier desserts, better suited to a lunch or dinner of fewer courses, are bread, farina, rice, or noodle puddings, often with raisins, nuts, or apples tucked into them. Cheese, so often eaten as a hearty snack, and even eaten at breakfast time in Germany, is seldom served after dinner as in France or the Mediterranean countries. However, semisoft *Tilsiter*, *Emmenthal*, or *Münster*, or the more notorious *Limburger*, might finish off a light lunch or supper.

Caraway-flavored *Kümmel* or slightly sweet fruit brandy distilled from raspberries, pears, plums, or blackberries may be served after dinner on more formal occasions. *Asbach*, which comes from the region of the Rhine and is distilled from wine, is Germany's most famous brandy.

Coffee is a much more popular beverage than tea in Germany. This is not surprising in the land of the *Kaffeeklatsch*, that amiable custom of combining coffee, cake, and sociality. The damp, chill climate of northern Germany does, however, seem to encourage the taste for tea. This is especially true on Germany's East Frisian Islands in the North Sea. Since this is also dairy country, tea is brewed very strong in these parts and is taken with heavy sweet cream.

To go to bed soon after dinner would be a mistake for the German *Feinschmecker* (gourmet or epicure), for he might miss some special treat at the sixth meal of the day. This snack, taken between 11 P.M. and midnight, can be anything from cake or sandwiches to *Wurst,* cheese, or goulash soup. It is really *Brotzeit* all over again. These small and not so small snacks are referred to in Germany as *kleine Imbisse,* small "bites."

German towns and cities offer a variety of restaurants for snacks or complete meals. The *Schnell Imbiss* establishment, the place for a quick bite, usually has counters at which one stands while eating. The *Konditorei* has the coffeehouse atmosphere for generally light but more leisurely eating or sipping. The *Bierstube* is a modest, tavernlike restaurant for beer and simple, inexpensive food. The *Brauhaus* is similar but much larger. The *Weinstube* is a modest wine tavern while the *Weinhaus* or *Weinrestaurant* is somewhat more formal, concentrating on dishes that go well with wine.

The *Rathauskeller* or *Ratskeller* is a very old institution that had its origin in the German cities of the Middle Ages. Actually the *Ratskeller* is the cellar or basement-level restaurant of the *Rathaus* (town hall). It was designed as a place for the town officials to eat. Prices were very nominal at most *Ratskellern,* and the value excellent, so that they soon began to draw patrons from all over the town as well as visitors from other cities. *Ratskellern* are still among today's most popular eating places in German cities.

GERMAN INFLUENCES ON AMERICAN COOKERY

In discussing German food one cannot fail to note that the over-all character of cookery in the United States is more closely related to that of Germany than to that of any other European country.

While pockets of southern Italian, eastern European, Spanish, French, and Scandinavian cookery are easily spotted in the United States, it was the nineteenth-century German immigrants who established the broad pattern of American cuisine. Their influence emanated largely from the region that lay between Ohio and the Plains states, where most of them settled.

Some two centuries earlier, in the late seventeenth century, the Pennsylvania Dutch country had been settled by German immigrants. While a lively German-based cookery developed in that small region, the Pennsylvania Dutch (really *Deutsch*) cuisine remained local and contained owing to the strong religious beliefs, close family ties, and isolated way of life of the Pennsylvania German folk.

But the results of the German immigrations of the nineteenth century were far-reaching. From the 1830s on, Germans began to arrive in the United States in large numbers. They left Germany because of economic hardship and political unrest arising from the industrial revolution and the drive for German unification.

In the northern half of the United States they discovered a climate and terrain very similar to that of Germany. The same fruits, grains, and vegetables; the same meat and dairy animals could be raised in the American Midwest as in the German homeland. A Mediterranean people trying to transplant itself to the United States heartland would not have had this advantage.

Important too to the German success story in America were the zealous German housewives, the thrifty, hard-working German farmers, and the enterprising German bakery, delicatessen, beer-brewing, and restaurant folk. A look at modern everyday food patterns in the United States clearly shows the German influence: meat-dominated meals with potato, noodle, or other starch accompaniment; the prevalence of beer drinking over wine drinking; egg-and-meat combinations such as ham and eggs, bacon and eggs, hash and eggs; the use of tart fruits with meats and poultry, such as pork and applesauce, turkey and cranberry sauce, ham and pineapple; the popularity of pretzels, jelly doughnuts, sour rye bread, potato salad, dill pickles and sweet-and-sour relishes, and the almost too obvious hamburger and hotdog.

Many Jewish foods known throughout the United States are adapted from the German, for nineteenth-century Germany had a large Jewish population. While the principal German cooking fats are lard and bacon fat, Jews substituted poultry fat, omitted pork from their diet, and evolved a distinctive German-Jewish cookery that holds an important place in American cuisine.

GERMAN FESTIVALS FROM CHRISTMAS TO MARTINMAS

Germany is a land of toymakers. Woodcarvers of the Black Forest and Bavaria have been fashioning delightful objects, from spinning tops to toy soldiers, since the early Middle Ages. The combination of German craftsmanship, imagination, and inventiveness has also led to the creation of countless fascinating mechanical toys. Therefore it is not surprising that Christmas begins early in December in Germany with a *Christkindlesmarkt* (Christ Child's market, or toy fair) held in Nuremberg and many other cities.

While the toymakers are presenting their products to the public for Christmas buying, German housewives are busy in their kitchens baking *Springerle* and *Lebkuchen, Pfeffer-*

nüsse and *Christstollen*. These are the traditional baked goods that have become Germany's contribution to Christmas in many parts of the world. The first three are cookies that may be made well in advance of the holiday, as they keep well and even benefit from "ripening."

Springerle are "picture" cookies. The rolled-out dough is impressed with the figure of an animal or with some other design, either by using a specially molded board or a special rolling pin to imprint the patterns. The dough is then cut into rectangles, each one a separate picture. The *Springerle* are sprinkled with anise to give them a slight licorice flavor, and are then baked.

Lebkuchen and *Pfeffernüsse* are spicy with ginger, cloves, and cinnamon. *Pfeffernüsse* ("pepper nuts") usually contain black pepper as well, and are shaped into little balls or "nuts" of dough. *Lebkuchen* are really gingersnaps or gingerbread cookies decked in white frosting. The *Christstollen* is an oblong, yeast-raised cake crammed with raisins, currants, candied fruits, and nuts, its surface snowy with sugar.

The legend of Santa Claus stems from the person of Saint Nicholas, who actually lived in the fourth century and came to be known as a bestower of gifts. St. Nicholas Day is still celebrated in Germany and in other parts of Europe on December 6, the day of the good saint's death.

One story concerning Saint Nicholas tells how he helped the three daughters of a nobleman who was so poor that his daughters had no dowries and could not marry. On three successive nights Saint Nicholas went to the nobleman's home, and each night dropped a bag of gold down the chimney. Add some reindeer from Lapland, change the lean, ascetic Saint Nicholas in his bishop's garb into a fat, jolly, snowsuited gentleman, garble the name a bit, and you have Santa Claus.

German children in villages and small towns are apt to be visited on December 6 by Saint Nicholas and his black-faced assistant, Knecht Rupprecht. Good children receive a handful of candies and nuts. Those who have misbehaved can expect dark looks from Knecht Rupprecht, who ominously rustles his bundle of birch twigs for thrashings.

Traditional for the Christmas Eve meal in Germany is *Karpfen* (carp). It may be cooked with vinegar, raisins, and gingersnaps, or in wine or beer, or it may be boiled and

dressed with a rich, creamy sauce, or it may be prepared in some other regional style. Christmas dinner brings goose served with red cabbage and dumplings to the festive table.

Carp turns up again for supper on *Silvesterabend* (New Year's Eve). It is traditional in the first minutes of the New Year to eat *Berliner Pfannkuchen*, also known as Bismarcks and as jelly doughnuts, and to drink hot wine punch. *Pfannkuchen* really means pancake in German, but these deep-fried cakes are the exception.

For more determined revelers, New Year's Eve may mean *Katzenjammer* (hangover) the next morning, but by January 2 a new festival is already at hand, *Fasching*. Although Ash Wednesday and the Lenten season are still many weeks away it is never too early, especially in the Roman Catholic sections of Germany, to start to celebrate *Karneval* or *Fasching*. The word "carnival" is from the Latin-derived *carnelevare* and breaks down into *carne* (flesh) and *levare* (to raise or remove). Thus the "removal of meat."

The Germans make a big thing of saying farewell to the meats, fats, and other rich foods of which they are so fond. Bismarcks or *Berliner Pfannkuchen* also go by the names of *Faschingskrapfen* (carnival doughnuts) and *Fastnachts-*

kuchen (fast-night or Shrove Tuesday cakes) and are eaten almost constantly during the pre-Lenten season. In Cologne and other Rhineland cities, in Munich and in some Black Forest communities, the indulgence in beer and sausages, the parades and masked balls that begin to build up right after New Year, culminate in two frantic, blaring weeks ending in Mardi Gras, Shrove or "Fat" Tuesday.

To repair the ravages of Lent—and possibly to provide a spring tonic—the day before Good Friday is designated *Gründonnerstag*, or Green Thursday. On this day, otherwise known as Holy or Maundy Thursday, it is traditional in Germany to color eggs green and to eat green foods. A green salad, a green soup, or a cooked green vegetable such as spinach is very much in keeping for *Gründonnerstag*.

Meantime the *Konditoreien* are decorating their windows for Easter with giant, lavishly decorated chocolate eggs, fruited Easter breads, and marzipan creations that glorify the entire plant and animal kingdoms. *Osterschinken* (Easter ham) is served for Easter Sunday dinner, and it is accompanied by a green-pea purée.

April 30, the eve of *Maitag* (May Day) is Walpurgis Night, the time of the witches' revels on the Brocken in the Harz Mountains. In pagan times a festival was held to frighten away the evil spirits that, it was feared, might prevent the return of the goddess of springtime. During the Christian era this holiday became the feast of Saint Walburga, who was the daughter of an eighth-century Saxon king and who is believed to have brought Christianity to many of the German tribes. Since few Germans can get to the Brocken to combat the witches in person, most content themselves with remaining where they are and partaking of the first-brewed *Maibowle* of the season.

The *Maibowle* is prepared with white wine to which fruits, such as strawberries or peaches, and champagne or fizz water, are often added. The most important ingredient, however, besides the wine is *Waldmeister* (woodruff), a sweet-scented herb that grows wild in woodland groves in many parts of Germany. Recipes for *Bowlen* vary throughout Germany, but all of them celebrate the return of spring.

Bottled May wine is a light white wine flavored with woodruff.

The arrival of really good weather brings out the brass bands that keep things stirring in the outdoor beer gardens and the town bands that give nightly concerts in the parks. Of the many music festivals that take place throughout Germany during the summer months, perhaps the most famous is the Bayreuth Music Festival held in July and August at which the operas of Richard Wagner are performed.

Now too all the knapsacked hikers and mountain climbers, cyclists and campers appear, for Germans are wildly enthusiastic about the outdoors and seem to have retained their tribal ancestors' passion for nature. Those who prefer a holiday that is not too vigorous take off for the spas or "bath" resorts, where hot saline springs for both bathing and drinking are said to have curative powers known even to the ancient Romans.

Many of these resorts—Baden-Baden, Bad Dürrstein, Wiesbaden, Bad Homburg (this one gave its name to the Homburg hat)—were the playgrounds of royalty until the end of the nineteenth century. In *A Tramp Abroad*, written in 1880, Mark Twain was amused by the boredom of the wealthy, fashionably dressed crowds at Baden-Baden as they promenaded to and from the daily band concerts. People seemed to flock to the spas mainly to see and be seen. But, the American humorist admitted, some had come for a real purpose: "They are racked with rheumatism, and they are there to stew it out in the hot baths.

"People say that Germany, with her damp stone houses, is the home of rheumatism. If that is so, Providence must have foreseen that it would be so, and therefore filled the land with these healing baths." Twain goes on to describe one of the medicinal drinking waters: "For some forms of disease, the patient drinks the native hot water of Baden-Baden, with a spoonful of salt from the Carlsbad springs dissolved in it. This is not a dose to be forgotten right away."

Early September brings wine festivals to the towns of the Rhineland. Later in September comes the greatest of Germany's beer festivals, the *Oktoberfest*. Headquartered in

Munich, this festival extends into the early days of October, thus justifying its name. The first *Oktoberfest* was held in 1810 to celebrate the marriage of King Ludwig I of Bavaria to Princesse Therese von Sachsen Hilburghausen. The celebration has since been blown up to enormous proportions by the frankly commercial efforts of Munich's brewers.

On the Munich fairgrounds, known as the Theresa Meadow, it has become the practice for the city's breweries to set up huge tents capable of serving tens of thousands of beer-drinking revelers each night of the fair. The beer that is dispensed at the *Oktoberfest* is the first of the season's new beer, the beer that was brewed during the preceding March. Traditional accompaniments to the beer are spit-roasted chicken, *Steckerlfisch* (fish grilled on sticks), and sausages galore, especially the delicate, lightly cured *Weisswurst*.

Weisswurst is served hot, and there is a rule of mysterious origin governing the time slot in which it must be eaten. The hours fall between midnight and *Brotzeit*, about 11 A.M. At the *Oktoberfest* this rule poses no problem since the merrymakers stay up most of the night anyway.

On the first Sunday of the *Oktoberfest*, there is a huge parade with elaborate beer floats, marksmen, folklore groups, and dancers costumed in *Lederhosen* and *Dirndl* dresses, the colorful Bavarian costumes that are seldom seen any more even in rural areas except on festival occasions. The fairgrounds themselves are boisterous with entertainments, a fun fair, sideshows and rides, brass bands and dancing. There is a mass jollity that occasionally overflows into rowdiness. It would seem that nothing can top the *Oktoberfest*, and in southern Germany nothing does.

There is only one major holiday left before Christmas rolls around again. It is *Martinsfest* or *Martinstag*, St. Martin's Festival or St. Martin's Day, on November 11. St. Martin is the patron saint of harvest merrymaking, and it is traditional to drink new wine and to eat roast goose at Martinmas, although some German farm families slaughter a pig for this occasion. The Martinmas goose is stuffed with apples and chestnuts, and is served with mountains of sauerkraut and with potato dumplings—as always in Germany, good and robust eating, dear to the heart of every *Feinschmecker*.

Bismarck Herring

*

Gelbe Erbsensuppe   or   *Fleischbrühe mit Eierstich*
(Yellow Split-Pea Soup)   (Meat Broth with
                                          Egg Custard Cubes)

*

Sauerbraten   or   *Gefüllte Schweinerippchen*
(Marinated Pot Roast)   (Stuffed Pork Chops)

Rotkohl   *Sauerkraut*
(Red Cabbage)

Kartoffelklösse   *Salzkartoffeln*
(Potato Dumplings)   ("Salt" Potatoes)

*

Rote Grütze
(Red Fruit Pudding)

or

Apfelreis
(Rice Pudding with Apples)

or

Mohr im Hemd
("Moor in a Shirt")

Kaffee
(Coffee)

KIRSCHKALTSCHALE

(*Cold Cherry Soup*)

    1   one-pound can sour red pitted cherries
    ⅔   cup sugar
    2   tablespoons cornstarch
    ½   teaspoon cinnamon
    4   very thin slices lemon, with rind
    ½   cup dry white wine
         few drops red food coloring
         whipped cream, or sour cream with
         additional cinnamon and sugar

Drain cherries and reserve liquid. Add enough water to cherry liquid to make 2 cups. Purée about half the cherries, forcing them through a sieve or coarse strainer. Add purée to liquid. Combine sugar, cornstarch, and cinnamon. Blend with liquid. Add lemon slices and cook in deep saucepan until mixture is glossy and slightly thickened.

Add wine, remaining whole drained cherries, and enough red food coloring to give a cherry-red tint. Check flavor and adjust to taste. Soup should be quite tart. Cool and chill.

Serve *Kirschkaltschale* very cold topped with whipped cream, or top each serving with a spoonful of sour cream sprinkled with cinnamon and sugar, ½ teaspoon cinnamon to 2 tablespoons sugar. Makes 4 to 5 servings.

DEUTSCHES "BEEFSTEAK"

(*German Hamburger*)

    1½   tablespoons butter or other flavorful fat
    1   medium Bermuda or other sweet onion, sliced
          and separated into rings
    1¼   pounds ground beef, preferably neck and tenderloin
    1   egg, beaten
    2   teaspoons grated onion
    2   teaspoons minced fresh parsley

¾   teaspoon salt
     dash pepper
2   tablespoons flour
1   tablespoon melted butter
     butter or other flavorful fat for frying
     flour for dredging

Melt the 1½ tablespoons of butter in a large skillet that has a cover. Add onion rings and sauté over medium heat until tender and golden but not brown. Partially cover in last part of cooking period. Remove onions from skillet and keep warm.

Combine ground beef, egg, grated onion, parsley, salt, and pepper, and blend well. Add flour and melted butter. Mix through, taste for seasoning, and shape into 4 thick oval patties.

If necessary add 1 tablespoon more of butter or other fat to skillet. Heat fat to sizzling. Coat one side of each hamburger lightly with flour and place in skillet, floured side down. Fry at medium high heat until crisp and brown on bottom. Turn, lower heat to medium low, and fry about 5 minutes uncovered. Then cover skillet, leaving lid slightly askew to prevent steam from accumulating. Continue frying on very low heat until hamburgers reach desired degree of doneness. Serve topped with sautéed onion rings. Makes 4 servings.

SAUERBRATEN

(Marinated Pot Roast)

5   pound boneless rump of beef
     coarse salt

Marinade

2½   cups white vinegar
2½   cups water
1   medium large onion, sliced thin
2   teaspoons mixed pickling spices

1   teaspoon crumbled bay leaf
½   teaspoon whole cloves
¼   teaspoon whole peppercorns

2   tablespoons butter or bacon fat
3   medium onions, cut up
1   teaspoon salt
½   cup crushed gingersnaps
3   tablespoons butter
⅓   cup sugar
2½   tablespoons flour
⅓   cup white raisins
2   tablespoons sour cream (optional)

Sauerbraten may be prepared with top or bottom beef round, but boneless rump of beef is the best cut to use. Rub meat all over with coarse salt. Combine marinade ingredients, bring to boil, and pour over beef in a deep pottery or glass bowl. Do not use metal or plastic. Meat should be completely covered by marinade. Cover bowl with plastic wrap and refrigerate for 3 days, turning meat at least once a day.

To cook meat, remove from marinade and wipe it very dry. Strain marinade and set aside. Melt butter or bacon fat in a heavy-bottomed 4- or 5-quart stewpot that has a tight-fitting cover. When fat is sizzling add meat and brown it well on all sides. Remove meat and set aside.

Add the 3 cut-up onions to the stewpot and brown. Return meat to pot. Combine the teaspoon of salt with 1½ cups of the reserved marinade and pour this over the meat. Cover tightly and cook on low heat 2½ hours or until meat is tender. Fifteen minutes before meat is done add gingersnaps which have been crushed fine with a rolling pin.

When meat is done remove it and set it aside. Strain gravy into a bowl. Melt the 3 tablespoons of butter in the stewpot. Combine the sugar and flour. Add to butter, blend, and cook, stirring, over medium heat until mixture becomes dark gold. Add strained meat gravy gradually, beating with a wire whisk to prevent lumps from forming. Cook until gravy is thickened, stirring constantly.

Add raisins, and sour cream if desired. The sour cream

mellows the gravy. Check flavor of thickened gravy. It should be pleasingly sweet-and-sour. Return meat and heat through.

To serve *Sauerbraten*, slice and spoon some of the gravy over the meat slices. Serve the remaining gravy on the side. Makes 10 to 12 servings.

KARTOFFELPUFFER

(*Potato Pancakes*)

3	large potatoes
1	small onion
1	teaspoon salt
⅛	teaspoon white pepper
2	tablespoons flour
1	egg yolk
1	egg white, beaten stiff
	oil or fat for frying

Pare and grate potatoes. Let stand in bowl 5 to 10 minutes and spoon off excess liquid. There should now be about 2 cups of grated potato. Grate onion and add to potato. Add salt, pepper, flour, and egg yolk. Fold in beaten egg white.

Heat oil or other fat to depth of ⅛ inch in a deep 9- or 10-inch skillet. When oil is hot add potato mixture by rounded tablespoons to form 6 oval pancakes, not too large. When well browned on bottom, turn and brown on other side. Drain on paper toweling.

Repeat, adding more oil as necessary until all pancakes are fried. Serve at once, or keep pancakes warm on a rack placed over a pan in a 200-degree oven. This will help retain crispness. Makes 20 to 24 pancakes.

APFELSTREUSELKUCHEN

(*Apple Crumb Cake*)

1½	cups sifted all-purpose flour
2½	teaspoons baking powder

¼   teaspoon salt
⅔   cup granulated sugar
½   cup butter or margarine
1   egg
½   cup milk
2½   cups pared apple slices

Streusel Topping

⅓   cup sugar
½   cup flour
1   teaspoon cinnamon
⅛   teaspoon nutmeg
⅛   teaspoon salt
3   tablespoons butter or margarine

This type of cake is called a *Blitzkuchen* (lightning or quick cake) because it is prepared with baking powder as opposed to the more traditional yeast-raised apple cake.

Combine flour, baking powder, salt, and sugar, and sift into a mixing bowl. Cut in butter or margarine to the size of peas. Break egg into a measuring cup, beat lightly, and add ½ cup milk, or enough to make ¾ cup liquid.

Add to dry ingredients, stir just until well blended, and turn batter into a greased 8 x 8 x 2-inch or 9 x 9 x 2-inch baking pan. Arrange apple slices atop batter in rows with slices overlapping slightly. McIntosh apples are recommended for this cake.

Combine dry ingredients for *Streusel* topping. Cut in butter or margarine. Then work with fingertips until moist and crumbly throughout. Sprinkle over apples. Bake at 375 degrees for 45 to 50 minutes. Cut in squares and serve while still slightly warm if possible. Makes 8 to 10 servings.

AUSTRIA

T o ROMANTICS everywhere Austria is the land of whipped cream and waltzes, of Tyrolean chalets and fountained baroque palaces, of winter ski holidays and summer music festivals. To Austrians their country is all this and much more. It is, in the words of the national anthem, *"Land der Berge, Land am Strome"*: land of mountains, land by the river.

The river of course is the Danube, for Austria has immortalized this stream which flows eastward across the northern half of the country. In former times the Danube flowed through Austrian territory long after it had left the easterly situated capital of Vienna far behind.

But that was during the several hundred glorious years of the Habsburg Empire, when Austria ruled all or parts of more than half a dozen European countries: Germany, Hungary, Czechoslovakia, Yugoslavia, Italy, Poland, and Romania.

At the close of World War I the curtain was rung down forever on the Habsburgs' Austrian Empire. When the curtain rose again it revealed a tiny, land-bound country hemmed in by countries that had once been its dominions. Austria's population shrank by the surrender terms of 1918

AUSTRIA

from sixty million to six million and she was left with the giant and costly bureaucracy of her not too efficient governing machine—and hardly anybody left to govern.

Nevertheless great riches were retained by Austria. The mountains remained, the Austrian Alps that swing out of the west and cover nearly three quarters of the country. In the Tyrol, in the extreme western part of the country, dairy cattle pasture in the green mountain valleys. Their cream is sent to Vienna to garnish pastries and to top off steaming cups of coffee with great puffs of *Schlagobers* (whipped cream). Rushing mountain streams supply the waterpower for more electricity than Austria can use, and mountain forests yield lumber, tar, and turpentine for the shipping industries of countries that have coastlines or at least outlets to the sea, as Austria does not.

The most beautiful stretch of the Danube was still that which flowed within the borders of Austria. Storybook castles and rich abbeys ornament its shores. Before the river reaches the commercial environs of Vienna, it passes through the Wachau district, which is noted for its grapevines, its orchards, and its delicate pastoral scenery. In the days of the empire, the Danube was a royal road on which the Habsburg monarchs sailed, or which they followed by a land route in gilded carriages when they went to visit their royal cousins in Bavaria.

Austria's superb musical heritage, the customs and traditions of her mountain villages, the architectural triumphs and lively intellectual life of Vienna were all left to her after the dissolution of the empire. And so was her *Gemütlichkeit*, that quality of charm, warmth, gaiety, and agreeableness that so distinguishes the eager-to-please, even flowery, Austrians.

But most tenacious, despite her territorial losses, has been Austria's spirit of internationalism. Vienna was for centuries the center of the empire, a conglomerate city in which a score of foreign elements met and fused.

In no aspect of Austrian life is this harmonious blending of individual characteristics more noticeable than in Austria's cuisine. Hungarian goulash, German pork and sauerkraut, Polish carp, Bohemian yeast pastries, Balkan stuffed

vegetables, Italian veal dishes, and Turkish coffee seem as much a part of Austrian cookery as the native specialties of Linz and Salzburg, Vienna and the Tyrol. Austrian cookery is in effect an example of culinary *Gemütlichkeit*.

The ancestors of the Austrians also appear to have been a gracious people, ready to accept the gifts of the ancient Romans and to apply the niceties of civilization to their own culture quite early in the day. While the Germanic tribes north of the Danube pursued their crude, warlike existence, the Celtic folk who dwelt on the banks of the river and south of it were already building a heritage that would absorb the best of the classical, Italian, and Germanic influences.

During the Danubian Bronze and Iron Ages, there were communities of lake dwellers in Austria as elsewhere in central Europe. At Lake Hallstatt in Upper Austria, archaeologists have discovered evidence of a society that grew grain and vegetables, raised livestock, gathered salt from nearby mines, and lived in lakefront houses built on piles.

FROM ROMAN GRAPEVINES TO TURKISH COFFEE BEANS

By 400 B.C. a western European people known as Celts were living in the Danube River valley and in the Austrian Alps. They were an agricultural folk who had learned to work with iron and were engaged in mining salt which they used in trade. Austria's "Mozart" city of Salzburg in central Austria is named for the salt mines in its vicinity that were so important in the economic life of ancient times.

The amber trade was also active during this period. Eastern Austria, because it was level country, was criss-crossed with amber routes that took Scandinavian traders from the Baltic quarries in the north to Greece in the south.

A much-traveled amber route led through desolate salt marshes and past Neusiedler Lake, twenty miles long, on the border between Austria and Hungary. Neusiedler, in contrast to the Alpine lakes of central and western Austria, is a shallow lake filled with salty water. Near Neusiedler Lake is the Austrian village of Bernstein. This is the German word for amber. No amber is to be found in or near Bernstein, but the town's name commemorates the "amber road" of ancient times.

During the first century B.C. the Romans penetrated Austria and set up a fort at Vindobona on the Danube. Later this outpost of Roman laws and customs with its baths and arenas became the city of Vienna. The Romans taught the Celts Latin and planted cherry and peach trees. They established vineyards and passed on to the native population the art of wine making. There were roughly a dozen self-governing cities in Austria at the peak of Roman administration. A Latin civilization appeared to be taking root in central Europe.

Then, in the fourth century A.D., events took place that brought great changes to the lands south of the Danube. Germanic tribes began to sweep down on Austria from the north. By the late fifth century the Romans had been beaten back into Italy, where they were to suffer further defeat at the hands of the barbarians. The Germanic tribes that settled in Austria mingled with and dominated the Celtic-Roman population. The Latin language disappeared in Austria and the evolving German tongue took its place. But the Roman wine-drinking heritage did not vanish and it has persisted to this day despite the German beer-drinking influence—and in truly *gemütlich* Austrian fashion, both beverages have attained a place of high regard in the cuisine.

It eventually became the custom for the owners of the

vineyards that lay just outside Vienna to provide benches and tables so that the townspeople who strolled out to the countryside might linger to taste the new wine, commonly referred to as "this year's." The German word for "this year's" is *Heurige* and after a while the vintners' establishments came to be known as *Heurigen*. Their popularity became widespread in the early years of the nineteenth century.

Beginning in May, when the *Heurigen* opened for the season, the Viennese would spend their spring evenings and their Sundays drinking wine and eating sausages beneath the vines. At some wine gardens it was permitted to bring one's own food, picnic fashion, and simply order the wine to drink with it.

The *Heurigen* are more popular than ever today and may be found in wine-growing regions throughout Austria. Many of them have added music—an accordionist, a violinist, a zither player, a group of folk singers. Some *Heurigen* serve elaborate meals, have orchestras, and have even added imported wines to extend the somewhat limited supply of Austrian vintages. But perhaps the simpler, more rustic *Heurigen* where the patrons drink their wine *gespritzt* (diluted with fizz water) are the most appealing.

Most Austrian wines are white wines, although some good reds are produced. Since the output of Austrian wines is comparatively small, they are not widely available abroad.

Another Roman contribution was the establishment of fruit orchards. *Kirschwasser*, the brandy distilled from cherries, is as popular in Austria as it is in southern Germany and in Switzerland, where it is an important ingredient in Swiss fondue. When the Austrians are not drinking wine, beer, or coffee, they like the sweet, non-alcoholic fruit juices derived from apples, grapes, or raspberries which are known as *Apfelsaft, Traubensaft,* and *Himbeersaft.* Plump dessert dumplings frequently enclose plums, cherries, or apricots, and Viennese cookies, pastries, and *Torten* are more often jam-filled than not.

In A.D. 800, when Charlemagne was crowned emperor of the Frankish or "western" empire that was to succeed the defunct Roman Empire, Austria was incorporated into his domain as an eastern border province. Later, when Charlemagne's empire was divided among his grandsons, Austria was given its German name of *Österreich*, meaning "kingdom of the East."

Austria was ruled by a succession of dukes for several hundred years until the last of the ruling line died without an heir. At that point King Ottokar of neighboring Bohemia (now western Czechoslovakia) stepped in and laid claim to most of Austria, including the city of Vienna. Vienna and the eastern half of Austria might have remained indefinitely in Czech hands had not the Habsburgs come along.

The Habsburg family originated in Switzerland in the eleventh century. The name of their ancestral home, *Habichtsburg* or hawk's castle, was shortened to provide their family name. In 1273 the electors of the Holy Roman Empire came together in Frankfurt. It was time once again to choose a new emperor to rule over the conglomeration of lands that fell into the Holy Roman domain. King Ottokar was one of the contenders. Count Rudolf of Habsburg was another. To the consternation of Ottokar, Rudolf was elected Holy Roman Emperor.

Upon assuming his new office, Rudolf rode at once to Vienna to claim possession of this important crown jewel—and found the city gates locked to him. Ottokar refused to budge. Outside the thick city walls lay the vineyards and beyond those the *Wienerwald*, the Vienna Woods, a rolling area of wooded foothills that slope up in a westerly direction toward the Alpine ranges. Rudolf was not in the mood to camp outside the walls of one of his own cities and twiddle his thumbs. He immediately sent a message to the Viennese stating that he would reduce the Vienna vineyards to ruin unless he were admitted to the city without delay.

At the mere suggestion that the grape harvest would be destroyed and there would be no new wine to drink in the coming season, the alarmed citizens—so it is said—opened the gates. Ottokar fled and Rudolf entered the city. He had taken the first step in claiming the crown, always more symbolic than actual, of the Holy Roman Empire.

In an epilogue to Rudolf's seizure of Vienna and Ottokar's grumbling retirement to Bohemia, the two kings met in 1278 on the Marchfield northeast of Vienna, near the banks of the Danube. In the ensuing battle Ottokar was killed. Except for a few brief interruptions there would be no more nonsense about who would sit on the throne in Vienna: it would be occupied by a Habsburg monarch until 1918.

It has been said that other dynasties increased their domains by waging wars but that the Habsburgs did so by making marriages. By the sixteenth century strategic or fortuitous bridal arrangements had put into Habsburg hands the Low Countries, Spain, Bohemia, and Hungary (which included Croatia and Slovenia, now part of Yugoslavia). The Spanish branch of the Habsburg family controlled important sections of Italy and vast territories in the New World. It could truly be said that the sun never set on the Habsburg empire. It swept from the Philippines to the Carpathians.

But not even the Habsburgs were immune to harassment by the Turks. These nomadic Asian horsemen had taken Constantinople in 1453 (changing its name to Istanbul) and all the time had kept their eye on the plummy kingdoms and prosperous cities that lay farther west. They had defeated the Hungarians at the Battle of Mohacs in 1526, and by 1529 they were knocking on the gates of Vienna.

Advancing out of Istanbul in the spring of 1529, the Turks reached Vienna and pitched their tents outside the city walls. Meantime daring Turkish horsemen coursed along the Danube shores and made raids on cities far upstream in eastern Germany.

The city walls of Vienna, built with the ransom money Duke Leopold obtained from the capture of Richard the Lion-Hearted, were exceedingly sturdy and encircled most of the city. The Danube flowed along the unwalled portion, thus closing the circle.

The Turks had hoped to make short work of the Viennese, but the summer days dragged on and the Turks made little progress. The walls stood despite their bombardments. Meantime summer was drifting into autumn. In October an early snow fell and the discouraged and somewhat alarmed Turks broke camp and struck for home.

Although the siege was ended, the Turks continued to hold most of Hungary, and year after year they exacted tribute from the Habsburgs in return for permitting western Hungary to remain under Austrian rule.

In 1683, spurred on by rulers with highly aggressive policies, the Turks struck again. When word was received that the Turks were on their way, the Emperor Leopold I and his family, the high church officials, and the entire court fled to refuge in the west. This time the bombardment was fiercer and the Turks often came terrifyingly close to scaling the walls. The Danube route of entry to the city was also threatened and required constant vigilance and protection by heavy arms.

Meantime, within the city that dreadful summer supplies were running low. When food rations were exhausted, people turned to eating cats, and when Vienna's feline population was nearly wiped out, even less savory items found their way into the cooking pot.

In the end it was the Poles who turned out to be the heroes of the day. With characteristic Habsburg foresight, Leopold had some time earlier made a mutual defense agreement with John Sobieski, the king of Poland. On September 12, with the aid of other liberating armies, the Poles met the Turks in a fierce battle outside Vienna, routed them thoroughly, and sent them in rapid retreat down the Danube. This final reckoning meant the release of all of Hungary from Turkish control and the restoration of that country to Austria.

Another Pole to whom the Austrians were deeply indebted at the end of the Turkish siege was a man named Kolschitsky who had once worked in Turkey and who spoke Turkish fluently. In 1683 Kolschitsky was in Vienna serving with the Austrians. During the siege he had acted as a spy, and his accounts of the Turks' military strength turned out to be highly useful in the September battle.

When the Turks fled in defeat, they left behind them many well-provisioned tents of food, to the delight of the near-starved Viennese. But nobody knew what to do with the sack upon sack of hard little beans that the Turks left behind. They seemed hardly the right sort for making bean soup.

Only Kolschitsky, who had lived in Turkey and who had drunk many a cup of coffee, seemed to know what to do with the beans. He asked no other recompense for his services to Austria than the sacks of coffee beans, and with these he opened the Blue Bottle, the very first of the famous Vienna coffeehouses.

The coffee-drinking tradition was thus established in Vienna, from where it spread to the rest of Europe and throughout the Western world. Until Kolschitsky opened his coffeehouse in Vienna, most coffee had been prepared in the Arabic and Turkish fashion. It was brewed of pulverized coffee, water, and sugar, and was served in small cups with a thick layer of undrinkable sediment at the bottom. Although such coffee, thick and rich, has excellent flavor, Kolschitsky must have realized how uneconomical it would be to prepare the beverage this way, for only in countries where coffee grew could one afford to use so many of the ground beans per cup.

So Kolschitsky began to brew a somewhat thinner coffee, extracting the flavor by passing the water slowly through the ground beans. At first coffeehouse patrons, unaccustomed to the bitterness of Kolschitsky's brew, complained. But a dollop of whipped cream on top and a rich pastry on the side soon took care of that—and besides, people were beginning to develop a taste for coffee.

The Vienna *Kaffeehaus* soon became an institution. It was not only a place to visit for a cup of coffee, but also a club-like retreat with a quiet, unhurried atmosphere, an ideal place for scanning the many newspapers and magazines displayed on reading racks. Although card games and conversation are also pursued in the comfortable, old-fashioned atmosphere of the Vienna coffeehouse, the rule is to engage in these activities quietly out of regard for the other guests. Large windows, handsome chandeliers, marble-topped tables, and upholstered chairs are the hallmarks of the traditional coffeehouse.

In modern Vienna the staid old coffeehouses of the imperial era flourish side by side with the glittering new *Espressostuben*, espresso bars imported from Italy since World War II, which feature chrome fixtures, neon lighting, and jukeboxes. Each type of establishment attracts its own clientele.

In the coffeehouse, the Viennese does not ask simply for coffee. He orders from among as many as fifty differently prepared kinds of coffee, depending on the time of day and on his personal preferences. His choice, not only as breakfast coffee, may be a *Melange* of half coffee, half hot milk, or a variation of this type ranging in tone from a *Schale licht* (light bowl) to a *Schale braun* (brown bowl). A *kleine Mokka* is a small cup of black after-dinner coffee to which the Viennese generally adds a good deal of sugar. Turkish coffee, brewed thick, black, and sweet, is customarily served with another Turkish holdover, a square of the chewy candy known as Turkish delight.

But the brew that is most closely associated with Vienna is *Kaffee mit Schlag* (with whipped cream). Even more recklessly Viennese is *Doppelschlag* (double whipped cream). An *Einspänner*, literally a one-horse carriage, is hot black coffee served in a glass with a giant puff of whipped cream on top.

Just as in the early days at the Blue Bottle, Viennese coffeehouses serve a glass of cold water with every order of coffee regardless of type. Water is traditionally served with Turkish coffee, both in Turkey and abroad, because of its sweetness. Kolschitsky carried on this tradition in serving his thinly brewed coffee, possibly to alleviate the bitter aftertaste which troubled his early patrons.

Pastries are offered in Vienna's coffeehouses, and especially opulent and varied are the offerings of the *Konditoreien* of which several in Vienna are world-famous. Many women patronize the *Konditoreien* during the daily coffee hour between three and five in the afternoon. This sinfully pleasant afternoon dalliance among the calories is known in Austria as *Jause* (pronounced yow-zeh). The word really means afternoon tea, but the beverage is most often coffee,

occasionally chocolate. Accompanying the cake or pastry ordered from the *Mehlspeis Fraulein* (pastry waitress), there always arrives a side dish of whipped cream with which to embellish the confectionery further. Light lunches and between-meal snacks such as open sandwiches, soufflés, and creamed or delicate grilled dishes may also be had at the *Konditorei*.

The retreating Turks of 1683 left more than coffee beans behind in Vienna. Their presence outside the city walls was not to be forgotten, for Vienna bakers soon fashioned a crisp, delicate crescent-shaped roll called a *Kipfel* in memory of the would-be conquerors. The star and the crescent were the symbol of the Turkish Empire. They appear on the Turkish flag today and are also the insignia of many other Moslem countries. Sweet versions of the *Kipfel* also evolved. These were prepared with yeast dough or with a crisp buttery pastry and were filled with raisins and chopped nuts, sugar, and cinnamon.

Another memento of the victory over the Turks is the *Gugelhupf* cake which is baked in a Turk's head mold, a bulbous fluted pan with a center tube. The shape of the baked *Gugelhupf* resembles that of a Turkish turban. There are sponge-cake *Gugelhupfen*, and pound- and marble-cake types, but the classic *Gugelhupf* is a rich, yeast-raised cake dotted with raisins and currants and coated with sliced almonds. Many an economy-minded student or tourist has rounded out the day in Vienna with a richly satisfying evening repast of coffee and *Gugelhupf*.

Also a gift from the Turks, largely the result of their 150-year occupation of Hungary, is strudel. Strudel dough was earlier a Byzantine product used in making the many-layered, nut-filled and syrup-drenched pastries of the Middle East. The Hungarians adapted this flaky dough by rolling it up around apple, cherry, cheese, poppy seed and other fillings.

Austrians learned to make *ausgezogener* (pulled-out) strudel dough from the Hungarians, who excelled at the difficult task of pulling the pastry as thin as possible without tearing it. Ideally, strudel dough should be stretched to a semitransparency that would permit the reading of fine print through a single layer. Austrians also bake a heartier, less delicate version of strudel using a yeast-raised dough.

DINING IN
IMPERIAL VIENNA
The victory over the Turks was not celebrated with coffee and bakery goods alone. Banishment of the 150-year-old Turkish threat brought a spirit of release and rejoicing to

Vienna and an expanded realm to Austria. The Emperor
Leopold I was determined to transform Vienna from a Turk-
ish-threatened border town to a glorious center of European
civilization.

Accordingly he chose Fischer von Erlach, a young Austrian architect who had been working in Italy, to translate
the new-found spirit of jubilation into flowing lines of stone
and marble. Von Erlach's graceful and exuberant baroque-
style architecture was expressed in a number of new buildings that were completed in the early part of the eighteenth
century. Principal among them were the Karlskirche (St.
Charles Church) and the new imperial summer palace,
Schönbrunn. Schönbrunn takes its name from the many
beautiful fountains (*schöne Brunnen*) that grace its extensive grounds. Ornately decorated within, also in the baroque
style, Schönbrunn had 1,441 rooms and 139 kitchens. Bath-
room facilities, however, were sadly minimal.

Music was the dominant art form in Austria of the
eighteenth century. Haydn was court composer and musical director for twenty-nine years under the patronage of the
Princes Esterhazy. The Esterhazy family, Hungarian noble-
men who had huge estates in the vicinity of Neusiedler
Lake on the Austro-Hungarian border, also left a culinary
legacy, that of Esterhazy steak, a beef cut braised in tomatoes and sour cream.

Mozart is honored by an annual summer music festival
in Salzburg, the city of his birth. Nineteenth-century romantic music began with Schubert and culminated in
Bruckner and Mahler. The waltzes and operettas of the pro-
lific Strauss family were Austrian popular music. It was
Johann Strauss the younger who composed that ode to
Vienna's river, "The Blue Danube," but this was only one of
the four hundred waltzes he wrote to which Vienna danced
its way through the 1800s.

The tender and lovely Christmas carol "Silent Night" also
came out of Austria during this period. It was composed by
the priest and the choirmaster of the church at Oberndorf,
a village near Salzburg, as "emergency" music for Christmas
Eve. It appears that the church organ was in need of repairs

and could not be fixed in time for the Christmas service.
With music by Franz Gruber, the choirmaster, and words by
Father Joseph Mohr, "Silent Night" was first sung in a
choral rendition that Christmas of 1818 at Oberndorf.

The Austrian Empire continued to prosper under Maria
Theresa, who came to the throne in 1740, and under her
son, Joseph II, who succeeded her. Although women were
not supposed to inherit the Habsburg throne, Maria Theresa's
place was insured when her father obtained the "pragmatic
sanction," an agreement among the crowned heads of
Europe that Maria Theresa would be recognized as empress
when he died.

Nevertheless there were protests at the time of Maria
Theresa's accession, and wily Frederick II of Prussia chose
that period of altercation to snatch away a piece of Silesia
in Austria's Polish sector. This move was the first sign of
Prussia's growing designs on Austria, and an indication of
Prussian strength. Maria Theresa herself had sixteen children, possibly to make sure that there would be enough sons
so that no further arguments would arise regarding the
Habsburg succession.

Most of the first half of the nineteenth century was known
as the Metternich era. Unsettling times caused the Habsburg emperors to place affairs of state in the hands of this
very conservative minister who was dedicated to maintain-
ing the status quo and suppressing the growing nationalist
and liberal movements within the empire.

Despite the political narrowness, the espionage, and the
censorship of the years from 1815 to 1848, Austria was
fairly prosperous. Vienna's growing middle class of independent craftsmen and small businessmen was comfortable
and contented. It danced the waltz, visited the coffeehouses
and the *Heurigen*, attended concerts and recitals of the
music of Beethoven and Schubert, and lingered in the outdoor cafés in summer devouring pastries or violet-flavored
ices. Gas lamps were installed on the streets of Vienna, and
the city became romantically illuminated after dark.

A writer of the day invented a fictitious character, a typical comfortable burgher whom he dubbed *Herr Biedermeier*,
and thus the Metternich era also was known as the Biedermeier period. A favorite dish of the day was *Wiener Backhendl* (Viennese fried chicken), tender young chicken
coated with flour, egg, and bread crumbs, and fried crisp
and golden in hot lard. *Backhendl* has been called the southern fried chicken of the south German lands. It is usually
eaten with cold accompaniments like potato salad and a
cucumber or wilted lettuce salad. It is often served in the
Heurigen with wine, but it is also good with beer.

The revolutions of 1848, which developed out of growing
nationalist demands and economic dissatisfactions, unseated
Metternich and along with him the sad, epileptic Emperor
Ferdinand I. Although beloved by his people, the gentle
Ferdinand was hopeless as a ruler. He is said to have gone
about muttering childishly to himself, and making a great
fuss with his repeated demands for dumplings.

Peace was restored after Metternich's departure from government, and Ferdinand's nephew, Franz Josef, then a youth
of eighteen, took the throne in the same year, 1848. He was
to be the last of the great Habsburg monarchs. Unlike the
gourmandizing Viennese, the young emperor ate very spar-

ingly and retained the slender military bearing of his young manhood until he became a bald and bewhiskered old gentleman.

Throughout his sixty-eight-year reign, Franz Josef's tastes in food remained as simple as his appetite was moderate. He was a conscientious monarch and often took his meals from a tray at his study desk—a small goulash, some cold sliced meat, or the Austrian hamburger prepared with milk-soaked bread and known as *Faschiertes*. For a real treat Franz Josef liked, in preference to all the elaborate creations of the royal chefs, the boiled beef dish known as *Rindfleisch*.

Boiled beef was not only the emperor's choice; it was and still is a great Austrian specialty. It is usually prepared with the beef cut known as *Tafelspitz* (tip of rump) and is always served with a piquant sauce prepared with dill or horse-radish, capers or anchovies. Boiled vegetables and a tangy beet salad, sweet-and-sour red cabbage or hot green cabbage are typical accompaniments to *Tafelspitz*.

While the emperor pursued his almost maddening indifference to rich and abundant eating, the palace chefs continued to prepare elegant dishes to impress foreign dignitaries and to meet the expectations of the Viennese populace as to what the royal kitchens ought to put forth.

There was *Schaum Torte*, an immense cloud of fruits and whipped cream nesting in a large baked meringue, or between layers of meringue, that had been prepared with numerous egg whites beaten stiff with sugar.

There were *Zwetschkenknödel* (plum dumplings) made with plump fresh plums, their pits removed and the centers filled with lumps of sugar or with blanched almonds. The plums were then wrapped in batter, cooked in boiling water, slathered with butter, and rolled in sugar and cinnamon mixed with ground poppy seeds or with bread crumbs. For the even richer fritter-like version, the plums were dipped in batter prepared with wine or beer, which makes for lightness in the cooked dumpling but does not leave a marked flavor. Then they were fried quickly in deep fat, dusted with sugar and grated chocolate, and served hot.

Even the Viennese realize that plum dumplings make a

rather heavy dessert, so they are generally served as a fol-
low-up to a "light" luncheon or supper whose main course
consists of goulash soup or of thick lentil, bean, or split-pea
soup with smoked pork. The same is true for other kinds of
fruit-filled dumplings such as the popular *Marillenknödel*
(apricot dumplings).

Another dessert that is only a little less hearty is *Kaiserschmarrn*, emperor's omelet, which was created for a predecessor of Franz Josef. A *Schmarrn* is a thick, puffy, egg-rich
pancake that is diced or shredded with two forks during the
last part of the cooking. The word *Schmarrn* really means
cut or slash. The pancake-omelet is sprinkled with sugar
and cinnamon and is usually served with stewed fruit or a
fruit sauce. Traditionally, the *Kaiserschmarrn* is tossed with
sugared, rum-soaked raisins just before serving.

Franz Josef's wife, the Empress Elisabeth, was one of the
most beautiful women of her day and even more figure-
conscious than her husband. Despite her Bavarian upbring-
ing and the reckless eating habits of the court, the nobility,
and the bourgeoisie, Elisabeth disdained rich foods and over-
eating. To the shock and dismay of those around her, she
dieted constantly and, like a woman of the twentieth century
rather than one of the nineteenth, she lived principally on
beef bouillon, raw vegetables, cold milk, and fruit ices.
Elisabeth remained erect and slender until her death in the
closing years of the century.

For most Austrians, however, eating was a six-times-a-
day ritual. *Frühstück* in Vienna meant *Kaffee mit Milch* and
crisp, fragrant *Kipfel* or other white rolls with butter and
jam. Between 10 and 11 A.M., hunger struck again. It was
time for *Gabelfrühstück*, "fork breakfast," a midmorning
meal that might indeed be eaten with a fork if it consisted,
as it often did, of rich thick goulash with crisp oven-fresh
Kaisersemmeln (kaiser or emperor's rolls). A more modest
Gabelfrühstück might be composed of sausages, cheese,
sandwiches, or coffeecake, and appropriate beverages, generally coffee or beer.

The midday meal at 1 P.M. was the most important meal
of the day. While the elderly Franz Josef dined in the palace

on his slice or two of boiled beef with dill sauce and wiped his mutton-chop whiskers in satisfaction, other prosperous Austrians plunged into a substantial feast.

One might possibly do without *Vorspeisen* at midday dinner, but soup was a must. *Rindsuppe* (beef soup, often the broth from a *Tafelspitz*), the basic dish, was garnished with noodles, rice, or dumplings, or with *Fritatten* (strips of pancake), or with *Backerbsen*, golden-brown fried dough "peas" prepared by forcing the batter into hot fat through a strainer with large perforations. A beef, veal, or chicken broth might appear *mit Ei*, with an egg poached lightly in the steaming soup. *Leberknödelsuppe*, with meaty, well-seasoned liver dumplings, was possibly the greatest favorite of all.

A completely land-bound country, Austria seldom tasted ocean fish in imperial times, and even with today's improved transportation the supply of truly fresh salt-water fish is limited. But Austrians ate fish nonetheless, for Austria was a predominantly Catholic country. Besides, there was excellent *Forelle* (trout) from the Alpine mountain streams, *Krebs* (crayfish) from mountain brooks, *Fogosch* (a white-meated fish) from the Danube, and the always popular *Karpfen* (carp) from pools and lakes.

As to meats, pork and beef were favorites, but veal was probably king. *Wiener Schnitzel*, the Vienna "little cut" or cutlet, is still the most famous Austrian meat dish, although its place of origin is certainly northern Italy, very probably Milan. Only top-grade milk-fed veal cut from the leg makes truly good *Wiener Schnitzel*. The meat is cut in large slices and is pounded and flattened to a thickness of one eighth of an inch. The schnitzels are coated with flour, egg, and bread crumbs and quickly fried brown and crisp on both sides, usually in a half-lard, half-oil mixture. Only a squeeze of lemon wedge is required for a final flavor touch. And, as with *Backhendl*, potato salad and a tangy cucumber salad are considered the most suitable accompaniments. Hot vegetables are not traditional with schnitzels.

Schnitzels are a family with hordes of relatives. *Paprika Schnitzel* is a Hungarian cousin, fried in lard and smothered in onions, cream, and paprika. *Pariser Schnitzel* is a light, delicate Parisian version sprinkled with flour and dipped in

egg; no bread crumbs are used. Austria's schnitzels are sometimes prepared with Parmesan cheese for an Italian touch.

Naturschnitzel is natural, unbreaded schnitzel, which has a light dusting of flour and is fried in butter. One of the stickiest tests for an Austrian cook to pass is the preparation of a proper *Naturschnitzel*. It is of the utmost importance to flour the schnitzel on one side only and to fry that side first. If both sides are floured, the second side will become soggy even before the schnitzel is turned.

Schnitzel Cordon Bleu is a veal slice doubled over a slice each of ham and cheese, fastened together, breaded and fried; *Holsteiner Schnitzel* is the north German version, topped with an egg fried in butter and garnished with anchovies and capers. Indeed, the variety of schnitzels on a Viennese menu can be dizzying, even unnerving.

Game such as venison, wild boar, hare, pheasant, quail, and wild duck were exceedingly popular on Austrian dinner tables in imperial times, for hunting was a great sport and most of the nobility kept extensive game preserves. Mutton might sometimes be used in a goulash, or lamb slices might do for a schnitzel, but on the whole sheep was not a much-used meat in Austria, nor is it today.

Pork-and-sauerkraut dishes, boiled, braised, or pot-roasted beef cuts, roast goose, and roast duck were and are as well liked in Austria as in Germany. Vienna is especially fond of its beef goulash adapted from the Hungarians. The Viennese version uses more onions than the Hungarian, and may omit the green pepper. Sometimes the Viennese add a touch of vinegar. Occasionally a fried egg or "bull's eye" is plopped atop each serving of goulash.

In Vienna, in imperial times, the spring vegetables such as spinach, cauliflower, and asparagus were eagerly awaited. Immediately on their arrival they were decked out in flattering but very caloric dress such as parsley butter, dill-flavored cream, golden sauces of egg yolk bespattered with bread crumbs or bits of ham or bacon. Spring was always an occasion for celebration, however, for winter meant cooked root vegetables, pickled beets, and sauerkraut.

Spring and summer salads of lettuce, cucumber, green

beans, or tomato were marinated in tart, vinegary dressings. The same was true of potato salad, which was never bathed in mayonnaise or in creamy boiled dressing. Twice as much vinegar as oil was the rule for salads, for Austria was not an oil-using country like France or the Mediterranean lands, where the reverse proportion is customary.

As one might expect of the lyrical Austrians, they have given their own name to the tomato. No longer *Tomaten* as in Germany, tomatoes have become *Paradieser*, the fruits of paradise, because of their resemblance to the apple. Similarly the *Kartoffel* becomes the *Erdäpfel* in Austria, and German fried potatoes are *Erdäpfelschmarrn*, a sort of Austrian pancake of browned potatoes and onions. In the United States these potatoes are called home fries or, when even more pancake-like, hash browns.

The Austrian method of cooking rice was adopted from the Turks by way of Hungary. The rice was prepared pilaf-style, first sautéed in butter and then simmered in just enough water or broth to make the grains tender. But the favorite starch dish in Austria was and still is the *Knödel* (dumpling). Among these, potato dumplings, bread dumplings, and flour dumplings are held in high esteem.

Semmelknödel (bread dumplings) are prepared with diced white Vienna rolls mixed into a dough of flour, fat, egg, and water. They are usually about as large as apples and, unless expertly prepared, as heavy as cannon balls. But when the dumplings are doused with a rich meat gravy or served in a thick steaming soup, nobody—at least in Austria—seems to mind if they are just a bit on the doughy side. *Nockerln* (flour dumplings) are smaller since they are dropped from a teaspoon into boiling water or broth. They are usually quite satisfactory served with gravy dishes.

Dessert, after a hearty midday dinner in imperial Vienna, was frequently a sweet omelet, pancake, or soufflé. After all, one could always save the cake or pastry for teatime and have the plum or apricot dumplings for dessert at supper time. *Kaiserschmarrn, Palatschinken* (jam-, nut-, or chocolate-filled Hungarian crepes), or *Apfelschnee* (apple snow: beaten egg whites blended with applesauce) were appropriately light dinner desserts by Austrian standards.

Later in the afternoon, when it came to *Jause*, one could really indulge, choosing from an array of *Torten, Kuchen,* and *Strudeln*, and always with a little extra *Schlagobers* served on the side just in case one fancied more. Since this was before the days of baking powder, most Viennese *Torten* were leavened with beaten egg white. But, as the cakes always included such flavoring ingredients as chocolate, ground nuts, puréed chestnuts, pulverized poppy seed, and even grated carrot, they tended to be rather dense and not particularly light and airy.

Probably the most famous *Torte* of the nineteenth century was the cake created during the early part of the century for Prince Metternich by a member of the same Sacher family that established Vienna's famed Hotel Sacher. The *Sachertorte* is a rich, moderately spongy chocolate cake

spread with apricot jam and glazed with a dark chocolate frosting.

Imperial Vienna's eating day drew to a close with supper at 7:30 or 8 and very often an after-theater or post-concert supper at midnight.

During Franz Josef's reign, Vienna grew increasingly handsome. In 1857 the city walls, those bastions of the Middle Ages that had twice repelled the Turks, were taken down. The city needed to expand and, in any case, the old walls would be of little use against the new weapons the Prussians were developing. Since almost any occasion in nineteenth-century Vienna seemed to call for musical expression, Johann Strauss the younger wrote his "Demolition Waltz" to celebrate the leveling of the ramparts.

The Ringstrasse was laid out, a broad curving boulevard lined with trees and handsome new buildings, among them the Vienna Opera House which opened in 1869. Within the arc of the Ringstrasse lay the *Innere Stadt*, the old "inner city" with its Gothic churches, medieval houses, and baroque mansions.

In the 1870s the Danube Canal, an artificial channel diverted from the river proper, was completed, putting the Danube deeper into the center of the growing city. Between the main channel of the Danube, on the city's northern outskirts, and the Danube Canal lay the Prater, the city park, which is today distinguished by its giant ferris wheel.

In 1867 Franz Josef gave in at last to Hungarian demands for a new constitution and a separate parliament. The Austrian Empire now became the Austro-Hungarian Empire. Franz Josef was now both king of Hungary and emperor of the dual monarchy, and although Hungary's foreign affairs and treasury were still in Austrian hands, at least the Hungarian people had the national government for which they had so long clamored.

However, this move to strengthen the empire served only to illuminate new weaknesses. The Czechs were sullen at not receiving the same measure of independence as the Hungarians, some of the Italian holdings had already wrested themselves free and the rest would soon follow, and the south Slavs, although disorganized, were discontented and bitter. Franz Josef was not unaware of the growing problems of empire, but it was difficult to adapt the old Habsburg ways to the demands of the twentieth century. The emperor was not sitting on a throne at all; he was sitting on a time bomb.

In 1914 the Archduke Franz Ferdinand, Franz Josef's nephew and heir to the Austrian throne, was assassinated at Sarajevo in Bosnia (now part of Yugoslavia) while on a state visit. By means of an intricate network of treaties and alliances, the countries of Europe had long ago chosen sides. Now all were catapulted into World War I.

Franz Josef died in 1916 while the war was still in progress. He did not see Austria stripped to the bone after her defeat, nor was he aware that in the town of Braunau, on the German border in Upper Austria, Adolf Hitler had been born some twenty-seven years earlier.

Hitler learned much of his anti-Semitism while he was living, under conditions of extreme poverty and bitterness, in pre-World War I Vienna, where a rabid hostility toward the Jews had been developing since the 1880s. Hitler left Austria and moved to Germany before the outbreak of World War I. In 1938, five years after he came to power in Germany, he reached out for Austria, which he had always felt was rightfully his. The *Anschluss*, the union with Nazi Germany, once again brought Austria down to a crashing defeat at the close of World War II.

Vienna was ravaged by war damage and racked by hunger and disease in the immediate postwar years. However, today's Vienna, if not quite the world capital of the final great Habsburg centuries, has recaptured much of its former style and one can dine there once again very much in the imperial manner.

Nearly one quarter of Austria's population lives in Vienna. For the remaining three quarters, residing in the provinces and in other Austrian cities, life has a rather different flavor. Vienna is unique and not really typical of the rest of

LIVING AND EATING IN THE AUSTRIAN COUNTRYSIDE

Austria, not only because of its tradition as an imperial city, but because it lies in the flat eastern sector of Austria, the only region that is not covered by mountains.

In the western part of the country, towering among the Austrian Alps, is the 12,461-foot Grossglockner, the highest peak in Austria. Many mountains in this westernmost region, known as the Tyrol, are covered with ice and snow the year round. There is a great deal of glacial activity, and when the *Föhn*, the dry warming wind from the south, blows toward the mountains there are avalanches that hurtle down into the valleys and bury villages and roads. But the *Föhn* also makes farming possible in the high mountain valleys.

Innsbruck, set high in the mountains, is the capital of the Tyrol. In the twelfth century this city was a trading post. Today, with its steep-roofed gray stone houses, the narrow clustered lanes, and arcaded shops of its old town, Innsbruck still has an aura of the Middle Ages. Its most famous sight is the *Goldenes Dachl*, the Golden Roof, once a ducal residence and later the refuge of Maximilian I, who set up court there during one of those annoying intervals when a non-Habsburg held Vienna. (This was between 1485 and 1490 when Matthias Corvinus, the Hungarian king, enjoyed a brief reign in Austria.)

Maximilian added a sculptured double balcony to the old building at Innsbruck and roofed it with tiles of gilded copper. His greatest pleasure was to stand with his court on the balcony of his provincial palace surveying the glorious Alpine scenery or watching entertainments in the courtyard below.

Many farm and village houses in the Tyrol have balconies that, in summer, drip with the brilliant pinks, reds, and yellows of flowering plants. Most houses are built in Swiss-chalet style, with a steeply pitched roof that has a deep overhang to keep out rain and snow. The interiors are simple. A huge tiled stove on the first floor serves for cooking in the kitchen and simultaneously, with its closed side, warms the next room which is the family's combined living room and dining room, known as the *Stube*.

The *Stube* is wood-paneled, low-ceilinged, and cozy. It has built-in cupboards, benches along the walls, and a large wooden table for family meals. Few Austrian village houses enjoy the luxury of heating in the second-floor bedrooms, but the members of the family sleep blissfully under mountains of goose-down quilts.

In the tiny mountain villages one still sees men and boys in the short, suspendered leather pants known as *Lederhosen*, for they are long-wearing and almost indestructible. The full-skirted *Dirndl* worn with a white puffed-sleeve blouse, bodice, and apron is also seen on the village women and girls—and everywhere people are dressed in suits and outer clothing of sturdy woolen *Loden* cloth.

In the mountains meals are simple and hearty. Breakfasts can run to three and four a morning for those who waken early in brisk winter weather or, in summer, begin the round of farm work at daybreak. Foods like *Schrot* soup, a loose bran-and-milk porridge, or rib-sticking pancakes of potatoes and cottage cheese are served at breakfast time as are thickly sliced dark bread and butter, cheese, sausage, and mugs of coffee with hot milk.

For lunches and suppers there are thick soups of dried peas or lentils, *Tirolerknödel* (Tyrol dumplings with bits of smoked meat mixed into them), or *Gröstl*, a favorite Alpine hash of diced leftover meat, fried potatoes, and onions.

The city of Salzburg in central Austria has contributed its own specialty to Austrian national cuisine, a golden puffy sweet soufflé known as *Salzburger Nockerl*. This light, delicate dessert of sugar and beaten eggs just tinged with the flavor of lemon or vanilla is very different from the small flour dumplings that are also called *Nockerln*.

The city of Linz, which lies on the Danube about one hundred miles west of Vienna, is the home of *Linzertorte*, a jam-filled cake prepared entirely of buttery pastry dough that contains ground nuts and cinnamon. *Linzertorte*, served with the inevitable dollop of whipped cream on the side, shares honors with *Sachertorte* in Austria's coffeehouses and *Konditoreien*.

Also here in central Austria are the famous spas of Bad Ischl and Bad Gastein where the wealthy and fashionable of the imperial era flocked to take the waters. Bad Gastein first became famous in the fifteenth century when the Duke of Styria who was suffering from gangrene of the leg went there to try the reputed healing qualities of the springs. The duke's miraculous cure attracted ailing nobility from far and wide, and many enjoyed similar cures over the years. Quite recently it was discovered that the Bad Gastein springs are radioactive, a factor that may have much to do with their effectiveness.

Bad Ischl was where the Emperor Franz Josef had his summer court. Ischl's pastry shops had long attempted to rival those of Vienna since no effort was spared to please the royal taste. So it was that *Ischler* cookies, butter-rich rounds put together with raspberry jam and dipped in chocolate glaze, came out of this elegant watering resort.

Kitzbühel is probably today's most fashionable Austrian resort. Set in the renowned ski region of the Kitzbühel Alps in west central Austria, this town is a major winter sports center and a magnet for celebrities throughout the ski season. The passion for skiing in Austria is so great, in fact, that many more people are injured each year in skiing mishaps than in auto accidents.

Styria, the green and wooded region of southern Austria, is noted for its especially tender local breed of chicken which is traditionally served roasted on a spit. It is called *Steirisches Brathuhn*. And almost anywhere in the country regions of Austria one can find *Bauernschmaus*, homely but good farm fare that is really a boiled dinner consisting of smoked and fresh pork, sausages, sauerkraut, and a stout dumpling.

THE AUSTRIAN FESTIVAL YEAR

Soon after the New Year one may come upon a strange sight in certain country regions of Austria, a sight that is eerily reminiscent of Halloween. Through the village streets come men and boys masked as witches, ogres, wild animals, and fiends. Wearing weird costumes, they jingle bells, bang on drums, and make loud, frightening noises as they stamp about and run in all directions.

One wonders what this odd behavior early in January can possibly mean. To country people in Austria the explanation is simple. It is time to scare winter away, to serve warning that spring is coming in a few more months and that winter had better begin to loosen its icy grip. This ancient pre-Christian festival is called *Schemenlauf* (phantom or shadow "run") in some regions, *Perchtenlauf* or *Glöcklerlauf* in others.

January is also the start of *Fasching*, for the longer the carnival season lasts the better. There must be time for

ample celebration, and even two whole months is not too long. For *Fasching* means gay parties and balls, often six or seven in an evening in Vienna.

Each segment of society has its pre-Lenten gala social affair—bus drivers and street cleaners, artists and students, trade workers and shopkeepers. Those at the very pinnacle of the social structure attend the glittering Opera Ball in the Vienna State Opera House. The Opera Ball is attended in the most elegant formal dress, but many balls are held in fancy dress calling for masks and costumes.

Faschingskrapfen, jelly doughnuts, fluffier and crisper than the usual soggy product, are the traditional carnival food in Austria as in Germany, for they symbolize the using up of fats before the Lenten fast. *Faschingskrapfen* are eaten for the last time on Shrove Tuesday. On the following day, Ash Wednesday, Lent begins. It is solemnly observed in many parts of Austria with the eating of the *Fastenbrezel* (fast pretzel).

One theory about the origin of the word "pretzel" is that it come from the Latin *pretium*, meaning "prize," because in early Christian times these brittle baked knots of dough were awarded to deserving students by the monks who instructed them. Pretzels, with their intriguing shape that combines a circle and a cross, were originally made in monasteries.

Easter Sunday is one occasion in Austria when lamb comes to the table instead of veal, beef, or pork. Breaded and fried baby lamb slices often substitute for veal as *Wiener Schnitzel* in the spring.

With the arrival of balmy weather, the *Wienerwald*, the Vienna Woods with its groves and streams and gently sloping meadows, lures the Viennese from the city. The *Heurigen* which lie in the vineyard area between the city limits and the *Wienerwald* also begin a lively season. And in the Alpine provinces and other country districts folk festivals with costumed yodelers and folk dancers bring visitors from near and far.

As in Germany, the tall white-bearded Saint Nicholas in his glittering robes and spade-shaped bishop's hat visits village children on December 6. In Austria his assistant is a black-faced, horned devil called Krampus. In keeping with the St. Nicholas Day tradition the kindly bishop distributes candy, nuts, and dried fruits to the children who have been good, while just behind him in the doorway lurks Krampus, rattling his chains and wielding his switch, ready to deal with any young incorrigibles.

The day before Christmas is a fast day and the Christmas Eve meal generally consists of fish soup followed by breaded fried carp slices, pickled beets, potato salad, and *Gugelhupf* or *Linzertorte*. The manger scene is set out beneath the family Christmas tree with its homemade decorations of gilded and silvered nuts, paper chains, and holiday cookies. Late in the evening the entire family troops through the snow to midnight mass. For Christmas dinner it is traditional to have roast goose, potato dumplings, red cabbage, and Christmas cookies.

New Year's Eve brings the ringing of church bells, the exchange of good wishes, and the curiosity common to all mankind as to what the coming twelve months may have in store. In Austria, as in parts of Germany, fortunes are told on this night by pouring drops of molten lead into a basin of cold water. From the odd shapes the bits of lead assume when they harden, each person attempts to decipher his future. On New Year's Eve *Faschingskrapfen* are eaten for the first time, for the carnival season is again at hand. *Spanferkel*, roast suckling pig, is the thing to have for dinner on New Year's Day for it is said to bring good luck.

In the Austrian countryside Epiphany on January 6 is celebrated with a charming children's procession commemorating the pilgrimage of the Three Kings bearing gifts for the Christ Child. Through the frosty lanes on this night comes first a group of young carolers called the "star singers." Behind them walks the proud "star carrier" who bears aloft a brightly lit lantern in the shape of a star. And behind him, following the star that will lead them to the Child, march three young people dressed in the costumes of the Three Kings. On this night the Christmas tree is lighted for the last time. The Christmas festivity is ended, and already—on this very same day—the pagan festival of *Schemenlauf* is back again, and it is time to run masked and shouting through the countryside to frighten off the evil god of winter.

AN AUSTRIAN MENU AND SOME AUSTRIAN RECIPES

Leberknödelsuppe (Liver-Dumpling Soup)	or	*Fritattensuppe* (Beef Soup with Shredded Pancake)
	*	
Tafelspitz (Boiled Beef)	or	*Wiener Schnitzel*
Dill Sauce		*Erdäpfelsalat* (Potato Salad)
Erdäpfeln (Potatoes)		*Gurkensalat* (Cucumber Salad)
Karotten (Carrots)		
	*	
Apfelschnee (Apple Snow)	or	*Kaiserschmarrn* (Emperor's Omelet)
	Kaffee (Coffee)	

LEBERKNÖDEL

(*Liver Dumplings*)

½	pound calf or steer liver
2	medium size Vienna rolls
2	tablespoons butter or chicken fat
1	small onion, diced
1	tablespoon minced fresh parsley
1	egg, beaten
½	teaspoon salt
	dash pepper
4 to 6	tablespoons dried bread crumbs

Trim liver and discard skin and large veins. Break up rolls in large pieces and sprinkle with water to moisten thoroughly. Melt butter or chicken fat in skillet and sauté onion until golden. Add parsley and cook a few minutes longer. Do not brown.

Squeeze out excess water from rolls. Put raw liver, rolls, sautéed onion, and sautéed parsley through food grinder. Add remaining ingredients to ground mixture and chill 1 hour. Mixture should be just firm enough to mold gently into 1¼-inch balls.

Bring to boil 2 quarts of clear beef or chicken broth. Drop dumplings into boiling soup a few at a time, allowing soup to return to boil before adding more dumplings. Let dumplings simmer about 15 minutes. Serve in soup, 2 to 3 per serving. Makes about 20 liver dumplings; serves 8 to 10 using 2 quarts soup.

WIENER SCHNITZEL

1	pound large, thin slices of veal, from leg
	salt and pepper

flour
1   egg plus 2 teaspoons cold water, beaten
    fine dried bread crumbs
    lard or butter for frying
    oil for frying
    lemon slices

Trim meat carefully and pound to a thickness of ⅛ inch. Sprinkle with salt and pepper. Dredge with flour on both sides. Dip in egg-and-water mixture and coat with dried bread crumbs. Let stand about 15 minutes at room temperature.

Heat equal parts of lard (or butter) and oil in skillet to a depth of just under ¼ inch. When shortening is very hot add breaded veal slices and fry to a deep golden brown on both sides, turning only once and being careful not to pierce breading. Serve immediately; garnish each schnitzel with a slice of lemon. Serves 4.

GURKENSALAT

(Cucumber Salad)

2   medium-large cucumbers
1   teaspoon salt
1   tablespoon olive or salad oil
4   tablespoons wine vinegar
1   medium clove garlic, put through garlic press
1   teaspoon sugar
¼   teaspoon pepper

Pare cucumbers and slice thin. Place slices in bowl, sprinkle with salt, and let stand 1 hour. Pour off liquid. Combine remaining ingredients, add to cucumber slices, and toss thoroughly. Chill well and serve with *Wiener Schnitzel* or other meat dishes. Serves 6.

APFELSCHNEE

(*Apple Snow*)

        1   cup lightly sweetened applesauce
      ⅓   cup apricot jam
        2   tablespoons fruit brandy or rum (optional)
        6   egg whites
      ½   cup very finely granulated sugar

Beat together the applesauce, apricot jam, and brandy or rum. Beat egg whites in a separate bowl until foamy. Add sugar one tablespoon at a time and continue beating until stiff and glossy. Fold in applesauce mixture and chill until serving time, preferably within ½ hour of preparation. Pile into dessert dishes and serve. Serves 6.

LINZERTORTE

        1   cup (2 sticks or ½ pound) butter
      ⅞   cup sugar
        1   tablespoon grated lemon rind
        2   egg yolks
    1½   cups sifted all-purpose flour
        1   teaspoon cinnamon
      ¼   teaspoon ground cloves
      ¼   teaspoon salt
        1   cup finely ground filberts, almonds, or walnuts
        1   cup currant or plum jam

Cream butter, add sugar, and beat until fluffy. Add lemon rind, and egg yolks one at a time. Combine flour, cinnamon, cloves, and salt. Sift together and add to creamed mixture. Blend well, add ground nuts, and chill dough 1 hour or longer.

Put two thirds of dough in an ungreased 9-inch loose-bottomed layer pan about 1¾ inches deep. Pat dough down evenly with fingertips and press it about halfway up the sides. Do not have dough too thick around bottom of rim. Spread jam evenly over dough.

Roll out remaining dough into an 8- or 9-inch circle, about ⅛ inch thick or slightly thicker. Slice into 8 strips about 1 inch wide and arrange these on top of jam layer, criss-crossing them in lattice fashion. Ends of strips should be pressed into rim of dough. Bake *Linzertorte* 40 to 45 minutes at 350 degrees or until edges recede from pan and top is deep golden brown. Cool, remove rim, and sprinkle torte with confectioners' sugar. Serve whipped cream on the side if desired. Serves 10 to 12.

SACHERTORTE

- ⅓   cup soft butter
- 3   tablespoons sugar
- 4   egg yolks
- 9   tablespoons sifted all-purpose flour
- 3   ounces semisweet baking chocolate, melted and cooled
- 5   egg whites
- 3   tablespoons sugar

Cream butter, add the 3 tablespoons sugar, and beat with a wooden spoon until fluffy. Beat in egg yolks one at a time and beat mixture with wire whisk until pale in color. Sift in 5 tablespoons of the flour. Blend. Add chocolate and blend.

Beat whites until frothy. Add remaining 3 tablespoons sugar, one at a time, and beat until mixture is stiff and glossy. Spoon one third of meringue on top of batter and sift 2 tablespoons flour over meringue. Fold into batter gently until almost blended. Repeat, using second third of meringue and last 2 tablespoons of flour. Now fold in remaining meringue very gently to blend. Do not overmix.

Bake in greased and floured deep 8-inch spring-form pan, at 325 degrees for 40 to 45 minutes or until center springs back to touch. Cool inverted on cake rack. Remove from pan and cut evenly into 2 layers.

Apricot Filling

- ⅔ cup thick apricot jam
- 1 tablespoon fruit liqueur, brandy, or fruit juice

Beat jam and liquid together with a fork. Spread half on bottom layer of *Sachertorte*. Place top layer over jam and spread remaining jam on top of cake.

Schokoladenglazur (Chocolate Glaze)

- 1½ ounces unsweetened baking chocolate
- ½ cup granulated sugar
- 3 tablespoons water
- 1 teaspoon butter

Melt chocolate in a double boiler. In a saucepan boil sugar and water together to a syrup that will thread when a drop is pulled from the tip of a spoon (230 degrees on a candy thermometer). This will take just under 5 minutes. Add syrup to melted chocolate and beat with fork until slightly thickened. Add butter. Cool to warm. Frosting should be thin enough, however, so that when spooned over cake it will spread slightly to cover jam.

Coat top and sides of *Sachertorte*. Leftover frosting may be thinned with a little hot water and swirled atop *set* frosting from tip of spoon to form border design or other pattern. Serve in small portions with a puff of whipped cream on the side if desired. Serves 10.

CZECHOSLOVAKIA

CZECHOSLOVAKIA brings to mind foaming steins of Pilsener beer, great racks of roast pork speckled with caraway seed, immense dumplings boiled in napkins, and steaming vats of prune jam filling for use in Bohemian cakes and yeast buns. Everything about this country seems hearty and generous.

The people work hard in heavy industry and on the richly productive farmlands. They play, it would seem, even harder —in vigorous, nationally organized calisthenic and gymnastic programs, the most ambitious in Europe. Czechoslovakia is a small country, only about the size of New York State, which burns with an intense concentration of energy. It is also the European country with the longest name and one of the shortest national histories.

Like Austria, Czechoslovakia is a completely landlocked country. The destiny of landlocked countries seems to be either dominion over their neighbors or subjugation by their neighbors. In Czechoslovakia's case, for hundreds and hundreds of years it was the latter.

From the tenth century onward, all or part of Czechoslovakia belonged to somebody else. Hungarians, Poles, Turks, Austrians, and Germans all held dominion there at one time or another. In fact Czechoslovakia did not even begin to exist as a political entity until after World War I. And even that period of unity and independence was short-lived, for in 1938 Adolf Hitler bit off a piece of Czechoslovakia and in 1939 he gobbled up the rest of it. Czechoslovakia was liberated principally by Russian armies at the end of World War II; it is once again a unified state and today it has a Communist form of government.

Czechoslovakia is the first of the so-called iron curtain countries and the first of the Slavic countries that one encounters on an eastward journey down the Danube. This is the beginning of that segment of the Danube that political observers call the "red" Danube. It is important to note, however, that there are political and economic differences among the various Communist countries in the eastern Danubian world, just as there are differences among the various democratic countries of the West. Each country has attempted to retain its individuality and to deal with its own problems in the most practical fashion despite certain restraints imposed on some by the Soviet Union.

The Danube flows only fourteen miles through Czechoslovakia; then it becomes an international boundary dividing Czechoslovakia from Hungary. If we think of Czechoslovakia as being shaped like a short, fur-topped boot with its toe pointing east, we can say that the Danube tickles the heel of the boot. Just before it reaches the instep, however, the river changes direction and dips southward into Hungary.

The boot itself is made up of three distinct sections that are also the three historic regions of Czechoslovakia. The region of Slovakia in the eastern part of the country is the foot of the boot. Its historic capital is the city of Bratislava on the Danube. Moravia in the midsection is the ankle. And Bohemia, in the western part of Czechoslovakia, is the ruff-like top.

The cookery and folk festivals, crafts and customs of modern Czechoslovakia are a blend. They combine the cultures of Bohemia, Moravia, and Slovakia; the Roman Danubian heritage; and the influences of the Germanic, Slavic, and Magyar border lands.

The region of Bohemia takes its name from the Boii, a Celtic people who lived there from about 500 B.C. In Moravia there dwelt another Celtic group whom Tacitus called the Cotines. Pre-Roman peoples enjoyed a fairly comfortable existence in the Czech lands, not only because of the rich farming soil and good forest lands, but also because of the presence of iron ore in plentiful quantities.

In the first century B.C., as part of their fortification of the Danube, the Romans began to build a twin city to Vindobona some thirty miles down river to the east. This was the city of Carnuntum on the south bank of the Danube, not far from the present site of Bratislava. Today the streets, buildings, and public works systems of Carnuntum are merely suggested by foundation markings on a bare, grassy plain beside the river. But in ancient times Carnuntum was an important outpost of Roman culture and a vital trading center on the old amber route that connected the Baltic region with Mediterranean Europe.

As in all the regions they colonized, the Romans planted grapevines in and around Carnuntum. Today Bratislava and its surrounding area of southern Slovakia is still wine-growing and wine-drinking country. But most of Czechoslovakia was to become heavily Germanized, and a great many Czechs do their leisure-hour drinking in smoke-filled beer halls similar to those of their Teutonic neighbors.

As in Austria, the fourth and fifth centuries saw the onslaught of the Germanic tribes into the Danubian region. The Romans were eventually driven back into Italy and the Germanic peoples took over the peaceful Celtic settlements in southern Czechoslovakia.

At about this time, too—during the fifth and sixth centuries—the Slavs began to make their appearance in the eastern part of Czechoslovakia. The Slavic peoples are believed to have originated in the area that is now western Russia and eastern Poland. There they had dwelt in rude log

FROM PRE-ROMAN TIMES TO BOHEMIAN PLUM ORCHARDS

houses arranged, for protection, in circular or horseshoe-shaped villages. The Slavs hunted, herded cattle and pigs, and, having little skill with metals, cultivated the soil with forked sticks. Less warlike than most peoples of their day, Slavs were often captured and put to brutish labor or sold like cattle. The word slave is, in fact, derived from Slav.

Recurrent waves of central Asian nomads had been driving the Slavs westward and southward for some time. By the 800s this unaggressive and rather crude pastoral people had somehow created a powerful and important Slavic state in Czechoslovakia, known as the Great Moravian Empire. It included Moravia, Slovakia, and Bohemia, as well as parts of southern Poland and northern Hungary.

To the west of the Great Moravian Empire lay the Frankish Empire of Charlemagne. To the east was the Byzantine Empire that had developed out of the old eastern branch of the now defunct Roman Empire. Charlemagne, anxious to claim souls for the pope in Rome, sent Frankish missionaries to Czechoslovakia to convert the Slavs to Christianity. The Moravian dukes and princes who ruled the empire reacted by asking the Byzantine emperor in Constantinople to send religious emissaries. And so it was that in 863 the Saints Cyril and Methodius converted the Great Moravian Empire to the Christianity of the East.

Unfortunately this great Slavic empire was not to be long-lived. Always at the mercy of the fierce nomadic tribes from Asia, the Slavs were overrun by the Magyars who arrived in Hungary in 896 and conquered Slovakia and Moravia early in the tenth century. So complete was the Magyar takeover in Slovakia that this region remained captive for the next ten centuries. Slovakia was not liberated from Hungarian rule until the close of World War I, in 1918.

Bohemia, the western region of Czechoslovakia, now began to rise in importance. "Good King Wenceslaus" of the English Christmas carol was a member of Bohemian royalty of the early 900s. He was not really a king but a duke, and his Czech name was Vaclav. He embraced the Christianity of the West and after his death became the patron saint of Bohemia.

Czechoslovakia's "golden age" was realized in the 1300s under Charles IV, who was both king of Bohemia and Holy Roman Emperor. Until Charles's death in 1378, Prague, Bohemia's capital, had the distinction of being the European city from which the vast domain of the Holy Roman Empire was administered. This city, today the capital of Czechoslovakia, became a medieval metropolis and a great center of trade and learning. The Charles Bridge with its handsome fortress tower was built across the Moldau River (in Czech, the Vltava), and in 1348 Charles IV founded the University of Prague. Craftsmen and merchants from Germany flocked to Prague and continued to populate Bohemia in the centuries that followed. The Germanizing influence was strong in many areas of Czech life, including that of Czech cuisine.

In the matter of *knedlíky* (dumplings) one might even say that the Czechs outdid the Germans. Czech bread dumplings, *houskove knedlíky*, are famous. They are prepared with day-old white bread, diced and kneaded into a hearty dumpling dough, then shaped into thick oblongs, three inches across and eight inches long. These dumplings are usually sliced with a thread, as cutting with a knife can create doughy surfaces. Bread dumplings are eaten with roast pork, goose, or duck, with stews or game dishes, and always accompanied by rich gravies or sauces.

"Tablecloth" or "napkin" dumplings are even more ambitious than bread dumplings, and are a distinctly Czech specialty. For these dumplings the bread cubes are fried in butter before being combined with the dumpling dough. Then the mixture is turned into a large wet square of table linen, the corners of which are knotted around the handle of a stout wooden spoon which is laid across the top of a kettle of boiling water. The napkin is tied just above the mound of dough to keep the dumpling round while it cooks inside the napkin, suspended in the boiling water. Other types of "tablecloth" dumplings are steamed rather than boiled and are extremely light. When ready to serve, the dumpling is stripped of its covering and cut with a thread or broken apart with two forks.

Of course there is no variety of dumpling the Czechs will not tackle—flour, farina, potato, cottage cheese, and an entire spectrum of feathery, yeast-raised dumplings filled with fresh or preserved fruit, served with melted butter, and sprinkled with sugar and ground poppy seeds or gingerbread crumbs, or topped with cottage cheese.

In addition to power, prosperity, and learning, Charles IV brought plums to Czechoslovakia. He was enamored of this fruit and imported the orchard stock for an excellent variety of prune plum from France. The plum yield was so high once the trees had become established on Czech soil that the Bohemians took to cooking the pitted plums with sugar into a thick jam or "fruit butter." Prune butter deliciously fills the centers of *koláčky* (ko-lach-kee), the small, plump, sweet buns of Bohemia and Moravia. Other fillings of cottage cheese, poppy seed, apple, peach, or apricot are also used in *koláčky*, and in the larger pan-size *koláče* (ko-lach-eh) which are cut into serving portions after baking. Besides furnishing the delectable centers of dumplings and sweet cakes, plums are put to many other uses in Czech cookery. They go into a tangy sauce for beef, a tart rich "black sauce" for fish, and into the distillation of a fiery brandy.

Jan Hus, the famous Czech religious reformer, was born during the golden age of Charles IV, but he lived to see the beginning of an age of almost ceaseless religious quarrels. In 1415 he himself was burned at the stake as a heretic for his criticisms of the Roman Catholic Church. His martyrdom brought twenty years of religious wars.

JAN HUS, CARP PONDS, AND BEER BREWERIES

Finally in 1434 a period of comparative religious toleration began. But by the 1600s new troubles arose. Since the Turkish invasions of 1526 Czechoslovakia had fallen mainly under Austrian control. By 1618 the efforts of the Roman Catholic Habsburgs to stamp out Protestantism in Bohemia led to a Czech act of rebellion. A group of Bohemian nobles threw some Catholic Habsburg officials out of the window of a castle in Prague. Defenestration—pushing people out of windows—was frequently practiced by the Czechs as an act of political violence, and although the Catholic victims were unharmed, the Austrian Crown took a dim view of such goings on.

War broke out, and at the Battle of White Mountain in 1620 the Habsburgs won a decisive victory. White Mountain was a dividing point in Czech history. After that, Catholicism became the state religion; Latin and German were taught in the schools while Czech, the native Slavic tongue, became a backstairs language. In addition the lands of the Bohemian nobles were confiscated.

The new nobility was Roman Catholic, and when not of Habsburg family stock, it was closely identified with that stock through friendship. Thus Austrians, Germans, Spaniards, and Italians took over Czech lands. While Prague became an architecturally splendid baroque city in the

1600s and 1700s, most Czechs now entered a bleak period in their history. Religious skirmishes continued until 1648 (the end of the Thirty Years' War) and Czechoslovakia herself remained a Habsburg possession until 1918.

The religious wars so decimated the population of Czechoslovakia that the landowners began to encounter a serious labor shortage. Little by little, since the 1400s, they had been converting their abandoned fields to other uses. Some were turned into cattle or sheep pastures while others, particularly the vast swampy acreages of southern Bohemia, were transformed into twelve-foot-deep ponds and stocked with carp.

Although Shakespeare in *The Winter's Tale* speaks of Bohemia as "a desert country near the sea," Czechoslovakia of course has no coastline. Yet as a predominantly Catholic country it consumes large quantities of fish as fast-day food.

As in Germany and Austria, carp is a favorite fresh-water fish. The Czechs prepare it in a sweet-and-sour sauce as do their Polish neighbors. The Czech specialty is known as *ryba na černo* (ree-ba na cher-no), fish with black sauce. For this dish the carp (*kapr*) or other fish is poached in a vinegary herb, spice, and vegetable broth to which beer, grated gingersnaps, prune jam or chopped cooked prunes, raisins, and nuts are added to produce a dark, rich gravy. The addition of sugar and lemon to the gravy provide sweetness and tang. Hare, in game-loving Czechoslovakia, is also frequently prepared with black sauce.

Many Czech landowners who were forced by the shortage of farm workers to give up agriculture turned to beer brewing, an enterprise that was to bring Czechoslovakia great fame. Plzeň (Pilsen in English) is a large city in western Bohemia and the center of the Czech brewing industry. The excellence of Pilsener beer is said to be due to the quality of the water of Pilsen, always an important factor in beer production. In the surrounding countryside the fields are planted with hops, which impart the slightly bitter flavor to beer, and with barley, which supplies the important malt base.

Still other landowners turned to mining and eventually to manufacturing. Besides iron ore and coal, Czechoslovakia is rich in sand and in clay used in its famous glassmaking and porcelain industries. Pilsen was to become the home of the famous Skoda iron and steel works while Brno, the historic capital of Moravia, became an arms manufacturing center and the seat of an important textile industry.

The Czechs were culturally as well as industrially advanced. Their composers and writers of the past century included Bedřich Smetana, Antonín Dvořák, Leos Janáček, Franz Kafka, and the playwright Karel Čapek. Yet, despite the restoration of religious and other freedoms under the Emperor Franz Josef in the 1800s, the Czechs never attained independent national status under the Austrian Empire as did their neighbors the Hungarians.

Nationalist feeling ran high in Czechoslovakia in the late nineteenth century. The Sokol movement, a combined patriotic and group calisthenics program, was set up in 1862 for nationalistic purposes, and was so successful that by the 1880s Czech had once again become the official tongue in most of Bohemia.

Czech troubles did not end with the unity and independence achieved at the end of World War I. In 1933 Adolf Hitler began to agitate for independence for the German-speaking peoples inside Czechoslovakia. These people were called Sudeten Germans because many lived in the area of the Sudetes Mountains in northern Bohemia. In 1938 the leaders of western Europe appeased Hitler by permitting him to take the part of Czechoslovakia he wanted. He called it his "last territorial claim" in Europe, a statement that turned out to be a grim joke indeed.

CZECHOSLOVAKIAN SPECIALTY DISHES

Czech cookery has a number of outstanding dishes. To begin at the beginning, the Czechs make soup out of anything. Meatless soups, for Lent or for reasons of thrift, are concocted from rye bread, beer, dried mushrooms, potatoes, dried beans, and the always popular caraway seeds. If meat stock is available, so much the better. But butter and flour, egg yolks and sour cream, and of course dumplings and noodles somehow produce hearty, steaming bowls of soup from kettles of boiling water.

Caraway goes with everything. It is sprinkled on pork, goose, and duck before roasting. It goes into soups and stews, and into Czech cabbage, potato, and other vegetable dishes. The use of sour cream in Czech cooking shows the Magyar influence. Mushrooms, which are used extensively, both fresh and dried, are stewed in sour cream, and braised meats are dressed with sour cream gravies.

Svíčková is the name for sliced beef tenderloin in a sour cream sauce subtly flavored with lemon or vinegar, onion and spices, and just a touch of sugar. *Svíčková* (svich-ko-vah) has a much less pronounced sweet-and-sour flavor than the German *Sauerbraten* and is in general a much more delicate dish. It is served with bread dumplings sliced into half-inch-thick disks, as is another Czech beef specialty, *Znojemský guláš* (znoy-em-skee goulash). This dish is named for the Moravian town of Znojmo which produces a dill-flavored pickled gherkin that adds a delightful piquancy when cut into and partially cooked with meat dishes. Znojmo gherkins are also served as a cold relish accompaniment to roasts, pork sausages, and the renowned beechwood-smoked Prague ham.

The Czechs eat a great many *brambory* (potatoes), prepared in dozens of ways, including boiled potato dumplings doused with butter, stewed potatoes cooked with minced onion, vinegar, and sour cream, and crisp potato pancakes fried in hot lard and topped with jam. Cabbage-family vegetables—kale, kohlrabi, cauliflower—hold first place in Czech affections, and both shredded green cabbage and sauerkraut are stewed or braised with sautéed onion and caraway seeds to make an indispensable meat and poultry accompaniment.

In eastern Czechoslovakia the most widely produced cheese is *brynza*, a sheep's milk cheese that comes mainly from the Carpathian Mountains of Slovakia. The flavor of this cheese is said to be due to the mountain herbs on which the sheep feed. When it is fresh, *brynza* cheese is white and sweet. It ages rather quickly and becomes crumbly and slightly sharp. At this point it is often made into the famous cheese spread known as *Liptavská brynza*.

Both the Hungarians and the Austrians have adopted this cheese spread, calling it *Liptói* and *Liptauer* respectively, but it appears to have originated with the Czechoslovakians who flavor it with onion, caraway seed, and chopped sweet pickles or anchovies, for a tasty mixture that goes well with dark bread and steins of Pilsener beer. Since *brynza* cheese is not widely available outside Czechoslovakia, a fairly good imitation of the cheese spread may be prepared using cottage cheese and intensifying the seasoning.

The Czechs like hearty salads that include a variety of ingredients and, especially, cold cooked meats. A *Český salát* (Bohemian salad), for example, might combine slivers of tongue, cold roast veal, Prague ham, sliced potatoes, finely diced tart apple, tiny peas, cooked vinegar-spiced celery root, and hard-cooked eggs. Vegetable salads of cabbage, beets, lettuce, cucumber, or tomatoes are preferred in tart, flavorful vinegar-base dressings to which sour cream is sometimes added.

When the Czechs are not baking their famous *koláčky* and other yeast-raised or short-dough coffeecakes, they show skill in preparing Austrian and Hungarian-inspired baked goods: crusty salt rolls sprinkled with caraway or poppy seed; buttery cookies laced with cocoa or ground nuts and filled with jam; fancy tortes; and pastries of paper-thin strudel dough. For everyday Czech meals, desserts may be as simple as stewed dried fruit or baked apples, or they may run to sweet omelets, fruit or cottage cheese dumplings, baked sweetened noodle dishes, or puddings or soufflés of bread crumbs or farina. The Czechs like coffee, but since it is rather expensive they often drink tea instead.

CZECHOSLOVAKIAN FOLK CUSTOMS AND FESTIVALS

Czechoslovakia has a continental climate of cold snowy winters and hot summers, for she is far from the tempering influence of the sea and her latitude is the same as that of southern Canada. While the land still lies locked in the icy grip of winter, thoughts have already turned to spring which is heralded in country regions by a procession of villagers carrying aloft small trees festooned with gaily colored streamers. Often the trees are evergreens, the symbol of everlasting life.

As with the "winter-scaring" festivals of Germany and Austria, the purpose is to hasten the departure of chill weather and to make way for the beginnings of the fruitful season. To make sure that winter will die, the village children often stuff a large burlap bag or other coarse sacking with straw. They tie it in the middle and paint a weird face on it. Then, near the end of the day's festivity, they trample the dummy to pieces and if there is a river or swift-flowing stream nearby they toss the remains into the water. This rite reminds us that in ancient times, after man had turned to agriculture and become dependent on it, a lingering winter must have instilled in him deep feelings of fear and insecurity.

Other folk customs and superstitions descended from pagan times play an important role in Czechoslovakian life, particularly in the High Tatra Mountains in northern Slovakia. In these mountains rises 8,737-foot Mt. Gerlachovka, Czechoslovakia's highest peak. Bonfires are lighted on the mountaintops on summer nights to ward off evil spirits— and many are the tales told of werewolves and witches and spirits of the dead, and especially of those living souls said to have vanished in the mists that frequently swirl down into the mountain valleys.

Of the many exquisitely wrought Czech handicraft products, the needlework seen in village costumes and household linens and the Czech Easter egg decorations are outstanding. Well in advance of the arrival of Easter, the women of the country districts may be seen in the towns offering for sale intricately designed dyed eggs that are the result of much painstaking work. Many village women use the batik method, first dyeing the egg a base color, then coating the egg with wax in the areas that are to remain that color, dyeing it again, removing and reapplying the wax, and so on until the desired result is achieved.

Traditional for Easter, which is known as *Velikonoční* or "great night," is the *mazanec*, a yeast-raised cake filled with almonds, raisins, and citron. A cross is cut into the top of the cake just before it goes into the oven. The *mazanec* is baked ahead, but it must not be cut until Easter morning —that is, the last stroke of midnight on Easter eve.

The Czechs celebrate Easter Monday as well as Easter Sunday. Traditionally the former is known as Whipping Monday, and village boys sometimes follow the custom of playfully threatening the village girls with switches, supposedly to rid them of their "laziness." In modern Czechoslovakia, Easter Monday is a day for open house, when anybody and everybody is likely to drop in. Easter greetings are exchanged, fruits and cakes are served, and numerous small glasses of potent plum brandy are downed.

Summer in Czechoslovakia brings massive government-sponsored outdoor presentations of group calisthenics and gymnastics inspired by the patriotic Sokol movement of the 1860s. Many Czech workers and other citizens repair in summer to the famous spa of Karlovy Vary (Karlsbad, in German) to rest, bathe, drink the curative mineral waters, and attend concerts and other entertainments. In the nineteenth century the Czech spas of Karlsbad, Marienbad, and Franzensbad were meccas for the fashionable international set. Of Karlsbad's many natural hot springs, the *Sprudel*, with its temperature of 165 degrees Fahrenheit, is perhaps the most remarkable.

The Czechoslovak Christmas season begins with the acquisition of the Christmas carp. This is an important family event in Czechoslovakia, even today and even in large cities like Prague. To insure having a perfectly fresh fish for the occasion, it is customary to buy a large live carp several days before Christmas and to keep it in the bathtub until it is time to ready it for the Christmas Eve meal. Catching the thrashing, slippery fish and killing it is a job that falls to the father of the family. It is accompanied by the shrieks of the children, generous bits of advice from the mother, and plenty of splashing water.

The ensuing Christmas Eve meal is naturally carp: carp soup followed by carp in black sauce, or a dish of fried, breaded carp steaks, or some other family-preferred preparation of this fish. For dessert there is stewed fruit or perhaps fresh fruit such as apples or even oranges. And all through Christmas there are holiday cookies. The spicy Christmas cookies of Moravia are especially well liked.

Once the Christmas Eve meal has been completed, the presents which have been piled up beneath the Christmas tree are exchanged. Family and guests sing Christmas carols and at midnight some families may go to a Christmas mass. Czechoslovakian folk customs and superstitions carry over into Christmas fortune-telling. One very popular custom is that of having each person slice an apple in half horizontally. If the exposed seeds form the outline of a star, good luck is in store for that person through the coming year. In the farm villages it is the custom for unmarried girls to bring a branch from a flowering tree or shrub into the house early in December and to place it in water. If the branch blossoms by Christmas Eve, the girl's good fortune will blossom and she will marry within the year.

Dinner on Christmas Day is a festive meal of soup, roast goose with bread dumplings, braised red or green cabbage, and Christmas cookies. *Vánočka* is the name of the fruited Czech Christmas bread that is traditional at. this time of year.

The medieval custom of cooking and eating the boar's head carries over into the Czechoslovakian New Year. In the old days the boar's head was the symbol of the successful hunt, and it has come to be an omen of good luck. In feudal castles the ears were lopped off the boar's head before it was boned, stuffed, and cooked. They were then replaced with skewers.

Modern Czechs content themselves with eating just the ear of the hog on New Year's Day, or preferably the boiled hog jowl accompanied by stewed apples and tart horseradish. Although hog jowl does not make the most tempting of holiday feasts, few people will risk a whole year's bad luck by defying custom and a deeply revered superstition.

Polévka se Žitným Chlebem
(Rye Bread Soup)

*

Vepřová Pečené
(Roast Pork Loin)

or

Svíčková
(Beef Tenderloin with Cream Sauce)

or

Znojemský Guláš
(Goulash with Gherkins)

Houskove Knedlíky
(Bread Dumplings)

Dušené Zelí
(Braised Cabbage)

*

Ovocné Knedlíky	or	*Koláčky*
(Fruit Dumplings)		(Filled Sweet Buns)
Káva	or	*Čaj*
(Coffee)		(Tea)

A CZECHOSLO-VAKIAN MENU AND SOME CZECHOSLOVAKIAN RECIPES

LIPTAVSKÁ BRYNZA

(Liptauer Cheese Spread)

½   pound sieved cottage cheese
¼   pound butter, softened
2   tablespoons sour cream
1   2-ounce can rolled anchovy filets with capers
1   teaspoon prepared mustard
1   teaspoon paprika
1   teaspoon caraway seeds
1   teaspoon capers
1   teaspoon minced or grated onion

Combine all ingredients, mashing half the contents of the can of anchovies and blending it into the mixture. Use the remaining rolled anchovies to garnish the bowl of cheese spread. Spread should be stored in the refrigerator but allowed to stand at room temperature about ½ hour before serving. Makes 1¾ cups.

VEPŘOVÁ PEČENÉ

(Roast Pork Loin)

3- to 5-pound loin of pork
coarse salt
1 to 1½   teaspoons caraway seeds

Rub meat all over with coarse salt. Sprinkle with caraway seeds. Put water in bottom of roasting pan to a depth of ¼ inch. Roast pork, uncovered, at 325 degrees for 35–40 minutes per pound. Add additional water to pan as it evaporates, and baste meat occasionally. Pan gravy may be skimmed of fat and thickened with a little flour if desired. Serves 4 to 6.

DUŠENÉ ZELÍ

(Braised Cabbage)

4 cups finely shredded young green cabbage (1-pound
    head, core removed)
3 cups water
3 tablespoons butter, lard, poultry fat, or bacon fat
¼ cup finely diced onion
½ teaspoon salt
⅛ teaspoon pepper
½ teaspoon caraway seeds
2 teaspoons vinegar
1 teaspoon sugar
  vinegar and salt to taste

Place shredded cabbage in a large pottery mixing bowl. Bring the 3 cups of water to a vigorous boil and pour over cabbage. Let steep 10 minutes. Drain off water.

Meantime melt 1 tablespoon of the butter or other fat in a large heavy skillet that has a tight-fitting cover. Add onion and sauté until golden brown. Add remaining 2 tablespoons of butter and melt to sizzling. Add drained cabbage and brown lightly, stirring constantly with a wooden spoon.

Add salt, pepper, caraway seeds, and vinegar. Cover and simmer over low heat from 45 minutes to 1 hour, or until cabbage is tender. If additional moisture is required add a small amount of hot water. At end of cooking period add the sugar, about 1 more teaspoon of vinegar, and salt to taste. Flavor should be mildly sweet-and-sour. Serves 4.

PEČENÉ HOUBY

(Baked Mushrooms)

4 tablespoons butter
¼ cup finely diced onion
2 teaspoons minced fresh parsley

     1   pound mushrooms, washed but not peeled
     ½   teaspoon caraway seeds
     ½   teaspoon salt
           dash white pepper
     1   tablespoon flour
     ¾   cup sour cream
     1½   teaspoons vinegar
           buttered bread crumbs

Melt 1 tablespoon of the butter in a skillet. Add onion and sauté until limp and golden. Add parsley and 2 more tablespoons of the butter. Slice and add mushrooms, and sauté lightly. Add caraway seeds, salt, and pepper. Cover skillet and cook on low heat 10 minutes or until mushrooms are tender. Add remaining tablespoon of butter and melt. Sprinkle 1 tablespoon of flour over contents of skillet. Blend in. Combine sour cream and vinegar. Add, and cook gently on medium heat about 5 minutes. Adjust seasonings.

Turn contents of skillet into a small buttered casserole, sprinkle thickly with buttered bread crumbs, and bake at 350 degrees for 15 to 20 minutes or until topping is browned. Serves 6 as a side dish, 4 as a main luncheon or supper dish.

KOLÁČKY

(Filled Sweet Buns)

     1   cake yeast or 1 envelope active dry yeast
     ¼   cup lukewarm water
     ⅜   cup milk, scalded
     ¼   pound butter or margarine
     4   tablespoons sugar
     ¼   teaspoon salt
     2   eggs
     2½   cups sifted all-purpose flour
     1   egg, beaten

Add yeast to water and stir until dissolved. To scalded milk in saucepan add butter, sugar, and salt. Remove from heat and stir until butter melts. Beat 2 eggs in a large bowl.

Cool milk-and-butter mixture slightly and add gradually to eggs, beating constantly. Sift in 1½ cups of the flour and beat vigorously with a wooden spoon until dough blisters. Add remaining flour. Dough should be stiff enough to knead. Add a little more flour if necessary.

Turn dough out onto floured board and knead until smooth and satiny. Place in bowl, cover, and let rise in a warm place until doubled in bulk. Punch down and let rise again until doubled. Divide dough in two parts, each to be rolled out separately.

Prune Butter Filling

½ pound dried prunes
½ cup sugar
   lemon juice or grated lemon rind
   cinnamon

Soak prunes overnight. Next day pit prunes, add water to cover and the sugar, and cook about 1 hour or until mixture is thick. Flavor with lemon and cinnamon to taste, and add additional sugar if necessary. Or use commercially prepared prune butter, adding these flavorings to taste.

Crumb Topping

½ cup flour
4 tablespoons sugar
4 tablespoons butter or margarine

Combine flour and sugar. Cut in shortening. Then crumble mixture with fingers until ingredients are well blended.

To shape *koláčky*, roll out dough ⅛ inch thick. Cut in 3½-inch squares. Place heaping teaspoon of filling in center. Bring both sets of diagonally opposite corners up over filling. Pinch to join all four corners and press down in center. Place on greased baking sheets. Brush with some of the beaten egg. Cover and let rise until doubled. Sprinkle with crumb topping. Bake at 375 degrees 15 minutes or until deep golden brown. Makes 24 to 28 *koláčky*.

HUNGARY

I T COMES as something of a surprise to learn that Hungary, the land of strudels, sour cream, and gypsy violins, has such things in common with the United States as cowboys, cattle drives, and prairie-flat plains. Of course Hungary is a small landlocked country in east central Europe, only about half the size of the state of Indiana. Yet more than half of it is a rolling, treeless grassland devoted to wheat-fields in the irrigated portions and to stock raising in the dryer portions. The *csikós* in his wide, calf-length pleated trousers and broad-shouldered decorated cloak may dress quite differently from the American cowboy, but his work is very similar.

In ancient times the plains of eastern Hungary, known as the Great Alföld, repeatedly attracted waves of barbaric horsemen from Asia. The plains were excellent grazing country for the horses and the herds of semidomesticated long-horned cattle and rugged sheep that the nomads drove along with them on their migrations.

The Asian barbarians were a milk-and-meat people. They drank mare's milk which they usually soured for longer keeping, they grilled the more tender cuts of beef and lamb and stewed the tougher portions, and once they were established on the fertile Hungarian plain they began to grow cereal grains as well. Thus the steaming kettle of rich beef goulash, mellowed with sour cream and accompanied by small tasty flour dumplings or tender noodles, is the heritage of the earliest invaders of Hungary.

Another feature of Hungary that attracted the Asian nomads was the presence of the Danube, which beckoned them toward the unknown but alluring West. The Danube is broad and placid as it flows eastward from Vienna, passes Bratislava, and serves as a boundary between Czechoslovakia and Hungary. Then, rather abruptly, it changes course and becomes a north-south river, dividing the Hungarian capital of Budapest and bisecting Hungary as well as it flows due south into Yugoslavia. Toward whatever westward point the Asian hordes rode in Hungary, they always encountered the Danube, a ribbon of temptation that they imagined would lead to even greener pastures.

The later Asian invaders of Hungary, such as the Turks, added to Hungarian cuisine those refinements of Byzantine and other Eastern civilizations that had rubbed off on them during their sweep westward: delicately piquant red paprika, tender, meaty poultry, flaky, paper-thin pastry. These were the basis for the paprikash dishes and the strudels that are found in modern Hungarian cookery.

Add a dash of Roman wine-growing influence, a sprinkling of Italian and French culinary refinements, a judicious ladling of Germanic cookery, and Hungarian cuisine emerges, the most intriguing and appealing in all Danubia. It is hearty yet seldom heavy, tantalizing without being spicy or otherwise abusive to the palate. Hungarian food, for the most part, is as lilting as Hungarian music and as varied as the changing moods of the gypsy violin.

ASIAN INVADERS BRING CULINARY GIFTS

The dawn of the Roman era found a Celtic people living placidly in the land that is now Hungary. As in Austria and Czechoslovakia, the Romans colonized the Celts of Hungary in the first century B.C. Particularly fertile and productive was the Danube valley and the gently hilly country that lay to the south and the west of the Danube. This region of western Hungary formed the Roman province of Pannonia. Here, too, lay Lake Balaton, the largest warm-water lake in Europe and an excellent source of fresh-water fish.

The Romans planted grapevines, fruit orchards, and cereal grains, making Pannonia one of the agricultural assets of the empire. But a gentle pastoral existence was not in the cards for the inhabitants of Hungary. The first of four major barbarian onslaughts from Asia took place in the late fourth century A.D. with the arrival of the Huns.

The Huns were a Mongoloid people from north central Asia. Their first adversaries in Hungary were the Goths, a group of Germanic tribes originally from Sweden. Pushing the fleeing Goths ahead of them, the Huns slammed across Hungary and used that country as their base of operations to terrorize Europe as far west as Gaul. However, with the death of their leader Attila in 453, their vigor diminished.

The next major invaders of Hungary were the fierce Magyar horsemen of central Asia, whom the modern Hungarians proudly claim as their ancestors. In their own tongue the Hungarians refer to themselves as Magyars. The Magyars brought the Hungarians their distinctive language, totally different from the Slavic, Teutonic, and Latin-based tongues that are spoken by their immediate neighbors. Hungarian is a Finno-Ugric language, and so the Hungarian's linguistic cousins are the people of Finland, and the Ugrians, a nomadic people of north central Asia.

The momentum that carried the Magyars into Hungary also carried them beyond its borders to eastern Czechoslovakia which they soon subjugated, and deep into the Christian world of the West where they met defeat at the hands of Otto the Great of Germany at Augsburg in 955. But the Magyars were sufficiently impressed with what they had seen of the Christian world to want to embrace its religion.

Stephen, the Magyar leader who converted his people to Christianity, was originally a duke of Hungary who in 1001 became the first king of Hungary with the pope's blessing. He subsequently became St. Stephen, the patron saint of Hungary. His birthday on August 20 is an important Hungarian holiday. King Stephen set up a strong feudal rule in Hungary that persisted through the Habsburg era and did not end until after World War II.

However, the conversion of the Magyars was not accomplished without incident. The Venetian Bishop Gellert, whom Stephen summoned to assist in Christianizing his people, was treated with especial savagery: he was put into a spike-lined barrel and rolled down the hilly slope of Buda (the western half of the city of Budapest) into the Danube. His statue stands today atop Gellert Hill overlooking the river.

The thirteenth century saw another invasion from the East, that of the Tartars under Batu Khan, grandson of the

ferocious Genghis Khan. The Tartars overrode Hungary and got as far as Vienna and the Adriatic before their energy was spent.

As a result of these successive invasions from afar, the cookery of Hungary was developing almost directly out of the Asian nomad tradition. The Magyars, who had learned agriculture in their years of migration from east to west, contributed a dried dough product called *tarhonya* which they had long used as a staple cereal food. *Tarhonya* is today prepared in Hungary by kneading a paste of flour, salt, and eggs, crumbling it into tiny pieces the size of barley grains, and drying these hard in a warm oven. It keeps indefinitely, as did the *tarhonya* of the nomads, and may be cooked in boiling water or broth like rice and served with meat and gravy. Or it may be sautéed in fat along with chopped onion, sprinkled with paprika, and then cooked until tender in liquid, like a rice pilaf.

The shepherds and cowboys of the Hungarian great plains prepare *tarhonya* to this day, drying the crumbled dough in the sun and cooking it as described. Also in the nomad tradition, and very much as in the early days of the American West, the Hungarian cowboy slices raw meat, beats it into thin strips, dries it in the sun, and makes it a part of his traveling pantry along with *tarhonya* for a ready-to-cook dinner. This dried meat is the Hungarian equivalent of American jerked beef or jerked venison.

Both goulash and planked dishes were eaten by the Asian nomads. They cooked their meat stews in large copper caldrons and fashioned horizontally cut rounds of wood from tree trunks on which to slice their grilled meats. The nomads carved a well in the wooden plank so that in cutting the slab of meat, which had been lightly spit-grilled over an open fire, none of the dripping juices would be lost. The modern Hungarian mixed grill is frequently served on a similar wooden plank or platter called a *fatányéros*. *Fatányéros* is also the name of this very tempting grilled main dish consisting of chops, sausages, liver, and kidney garnished with potatoes, pickles, and marinated salad vegetables.

Of course the Asian horsemen often ate their meat raw, for they believed the blood of animals imparted vigor to man. The Tartar hordes used specially devised tubes with which they regularly bled the neck veins of their horses, drinking several ounces of blood and then sealing the incision.

For a true Hungarian *gulyás* (goulash) certain basic ingredients and proportions are required, although family and regional recipes vary. The dish is always prepared with meat and onions and should be in the proportion of one onion to one pound of meat. Austrian and Czech versions of goulash tend to go heavier on the onions and often add caraway seeds. After the Turks invaded Hungary and introduced paprika, this spice became indispensable to goulash. Green peppers and tomatoes are frequently added to Hungarian goulash, and a few tablespoons of sour cream are frequently stirred in just before serving.

Goulash is usually prepared with beef or, in the country regions of Hungary, with mutton. The great exception is a dish called *székely gulyás* which is prepared with pork and contains sauerkraut, paprika, and sour cream as well.

A Hungarian stew that may have preceded *gulyás* as it is known today is the *tokány*, a dish prepared with meat and vegetables, but often using black pepper instead of paprika. Another stew variation is the *pörkölt*. The name means "scorched" or "singed" and is apt because the meat is well browned first and then braised with vegetables to yield a rich, deeply colored gravy. The *pörkölt* does not include sour cream. *Tokány* and *pörkölt* use beef, veal, pork, mutton, fowl, rabbit, hare, even variety meats, depending on the resources at hand.

But whether the stew be *gulyás*, *tokány*, or *pörkölt*, it should always have plenty of gravy with which to douse the varied and abundant Hungarian dough products. *Tarhonya* is the oldest of these, but once the Hungarian wheatfields were yielding a substantial harvest, the population began to enjoy many kinds of boiled pastes. Among these were *metélt* (noodles: fine, narrow, broad, or cut into small squares), *csipetke* (chi-pet-ke: "pinched" noodles, really torn-off nubs of noodle dough boiled in water or soup), *gombóca* (gom-bo-tsa: firm-dough dumplings), and *galuska* (ga-loosh-ka: soft-dough dumplings).

Just before the fourth and last of the great Asian invasions, Hungary achieved its golden age, the span of years from 1458 to 1490 during which Matthias Corvinus was king of Hungary. A typical Renaissance ruler, Matthias was a patron of the arts and of learning. From his own magnificent collection of books he established the famous Corvina library. Matthias was also crafty and predatory. He managed to grab most of Austria, ousting the Habsburgs from the throne in Vienna from 1485 until his death in 1490.

The third wife of Matthias Corvinus was Queen Beatrice, an Italian princess, and thus his reign saw the application of many Italian Renaissance dining niceties to the Hungarian table. Although the famous Hungarian cake, the *dobos torta*, was not created until centuries later, it is thought that the brittle golden caramel that covers the top of this cake is in imitation of the gilded foods that were fashionable in Milan, Florence, and other rich Italian cities during the Renaissance. It is quite possible that Matthias's queen introduced to the royal Hungarian table elaborate meat dishes, pastries, and other foods glazed or decorated with a thin leafing of real gold, as was the fashion in her own country.

Dobos torta, in any case, is a regal dessert composed of six to eight thin layers of spongecake, filled with layer upon layer of chocolate butter cream. The sides of the cake are chocolate-frosted and sprinkled with coarsely shredded hazelnuts, and on top goes the imitation gilding of caramel which must be scored before it hardens so that the cake can later be sliced into serving pieces. The name *dobos* derives from the cake's creator, a Hungarian pastry chef named Jozsef C. Dobós who died in 1928. But there is also a possibility that chef Dobós designed the cake's hard smooth top to fit his name, for the Hungarian word *dob* means drum.

Although the Turks had taken Constantinople in 1453 and were already raiding Hungarian territory in Matthias Corvinus's day, the powerful monarch managed to beat the invaders back. But after his death Hungary grew steadily weaker and in 1526, at the Battle of Mohacs, the Turks defeated the Hungarians. Except for a small western portion of the country, which fell to Austrian rule, Hungary remained in Turkish hands until 1683 when the Turks were finally driven out.

Turkish rule in Hungary was oppressive. One of its worst features was the practice of recruiting by force yearly tributes of young boys for the janissary corps; in Turkish, *Yeni Sheri* or "New Troops." Taken from their homes in the Turkish-occupied countries, these young Christians were marched away to Turkey where they were pressed into service for Islam and educated for war. Their families never saw them again.

During the century and a half that they occupied Hungary, the Turks saw to the cultivation of the paprika plant which was indigenous to India and which they had adopted during their migrations from Asia. Different from the Spanish pepper or pimiento, which was brought to Europe from South and Central America, the Indian variety has smaller pods and ranges in flavor from "rose," or sweet, paprika to sharp paprika. It is less sharp, however, than the fiery cayenne pepper. In late summer Hungarian farm and village houses are strung with bunches of paprika peppers gradually turning from pale green to crimson. Once they are dried, the peppers are ground into a rich red powder.

The Turks also brought chicken, a native Indian fowl, to Hungary. Combining chicken with paprika, the nomad-inspired sour cream, and onions lightly fried in lard, the Hungarians evolved one of the world's most ambrosial dishes, *csirke paprikás*, chicken paprikash. Hungarian noodles or *galuska* are a must with the creamy, paprika-tinged chicken gravy. Veal, too, lends itself well to *paprikás* dishes.

The Turks saw to the planting of apricot trees in Hungary. This fruit, which originated in the Far East, grows remarkably well in the intense summer heat of the Alföld, yet the trees are able to withstand the bitter cold of the extreme plains climate. Apricot preserves make a superb filling for *palacsinta* (pa-la-chin-ta), the thin Hungarian dessert pancakes, and apricot juice is distilled for the popular Hungarian *barackpálinka* (apricot brandy) and *baracklikör* (apricot liqueur).

The tomato, introduced to Europe from South and Central America, also took well to Hungarian soil and appealed to Hungarian tastes. Since the tomato has a limited growing season in Hungary's continental climate, the farm folk soon devised *lecsó* (lech-ow), a thick bottled preserve of tomatoes, green peppers, and onions cooked until tender in a small quantity of lard. *Lescó* is used throughout the year in preparing Hungarian stews and other dishes, and is also very good with eggs or with Hungarian sausages.

Surely the most impressive of the Turkish contributions to Hungarian cuisine is strudel. The Turks were the great culinary borrowers and lenders of history. From the Byzantines the Turks learned about the flaky paper-thin leaves of dough that were used in many-layered pastries crammed with ground nuts and drenched with honey or sugar syrup. These pastry leaves, which had been introduced to the Byzantines by the Persians long before the advent of the Turks, now were brought to Hungary.

The carefully milled glutenous flour produced in Hungary was and is particularly well suited to strudel making, and the Hungarians soon became skillful in pulling or stretching the dough. They then devised their own fillings of sweetened apple, cherry, cheese, nuts, poppy seed, and even fillings of stewed shredded cabbage. They rolled the tissue-thin pastry around the filling, baked it in long narrow rolls, sliced it, and so produced *rétes* (re-tesh): strudel.

The defeat of the Turks in 1683 freed Hungary from Ottoman rule but placed her completely in the hands of the Austrian Empire. From the early 1700s on, the Hungarian nobility flocked to the Viennese court, sometimes to agitate for Hungarian independence, often to enjoy Vienna's stimulating international atmosphere and to luxuriate in the growing splendor and brilliance of the baroque capital.

FROM AUSTRO-HUNGARIAN DINING TO EVERYDAY HUNGARIAN MEALS

During the reign of the Empress Maria Theresa, French influence was strong at the Habsburg court. French cuisine and French dining etiquette became fashionable, not only at the court itself but among the visiting nobility from all of Austria's subject lands.

By way of the Hungarian nobles, most of whom held large feudal estates in Hungary, French cuisine filtered eastward. It was now considered crude to use sour cream, with its barbaric heritage, in the preparation of certain Hungarian dishes; Hungarian lords instructed their cooks to employ instead heavy sweet cream, in the French manner. Similarly, lard, the traditional cooking fat of Hungary, was replaced by butter for more delicate flavoring.

Although pancakes are a very ancient and primitive food, the thin, tender French pancakes were surely the inspiration for Hungarian *palacsinta*. These nearly transparent, delicately butter-browned crepes, similar to those used for *crêpes Suzette*, are eaten as a dessert either folded or rolled around a filling of apricot, plum, or raspberry jam, or around fillings of sweetened ground nuts, cottage cheese and raisins, or chocolate.

In Hungary today, *palacsinta* are not reserved for grand occasions only, but are prepared in quite simple Hungarian homes and modest restaurants, for the Hungarian cook does not flinch at culinary operations that others might find intimidating or excessively time-consuming.

Stacked or layered *palacsinta*, called *rakott*, may be spread with one or several sweet fillings for a tall, cakelike dessert that is lightly baked and cut in wedges for serving. *Rakott palacsinta* with fillings of ham, creamed mushrooms, or creamed chicken, topped with a sour cream or cheese sauce, also make a very elegant main luncheon course or supper dish.

A native product of which the Hungarian nobility were especially proud, even in the face of French culinary accomplishments, was the excellent Tokay wine produced in northeastern Hungary near the town of Tokaj. This rich mellow wine, often rather sweet and hence served as a dessert wine, became known in the Austrian imperial court and throughout Europe as "the king of wines and the wine of kings."

In the first half of the nineteenth century Hungarian leaders became increasingly dissatisfied with Austrian rule. One of the most important figures of the revolution of 1848 was the militant Hungarian nationalist Lajos Kossuth. The Hungarian uprising was suppressed with a brutality not generally displayed by the Habsburgs. Still, the agitation for a Hungarian national parliament and a separate constitution did not cease. In 1867 Hungarian demands were granted at last by Franz Josef, and the dual monarchy of Austro-Hungary came into existence.

Despite improvements on the national level, the lot of the Hungarian peasant and worker was hardly any better than before. There was little industry in Hungary, and agriculture was still organized along the old feudal lines of King Stephen's day. Poverty and lack of opportunity led to mass emigration. The early 1900s saw hundreds of thousands of Hungarians depart for the United States.

Along with Austria, Hungary suffered defeat in World War I. She was stripped of more than two thirds of her territory, which went to the newly independent nations of Czechoslovakia, Romania, and Yugoslavia. The advent of Adolf Hitler found Hungary still licking her wounds. She was easily drawn into the Nazi camp on the promise that through a German victory her lost lands would be returned.

A second defeat, this time at the hands of the Soviet Union in World War II, led to the formation of a Communist government in Hungary. Collective farms were established, the existing industry was nationalized and greatly expanded, the country's economic health was improved, and some social services were offered to the people. Nevertheless there was deep resentment on the part of the Hungarian people at the imposition of many police-state controls. This led to the uprising of 1956, which although harshly suppressed did lead to some improvements such as increased availability of consumer goods and less obtrusive political propaganda. It is the unfortunate truth, however, that Hungary has not really known democracy at any point in her history.

In the years following World War II, Budapest, Hungary's

capital, was a drab, war-torn city totally lacking in the vigor and sparkle of the imperial era. Today, however, this city, divided by the Danube into the halves of Buda and Pest, is once again responding to the sound of gypsy violins. Coffee-houses and wine cellars abound. Margaret Island, a minia-ture world of green in the middle of the Danube, boasts rose gardens, swimming facilities, and outdoor entertainment during the spring and summer months.

Buda, on the west bank of the Danube, is hilly and studded with historic monuments. Pest, linked to Buda by eight bridges across the broad Danube, is flat and stretches away toward the great plains of eastern Hungary. Pest contains most of the capital's commercial, cultural, and educational buildings. On the shore of the Danube, in Pest, stands the impressive Neo-Gothic parliament building, with its great dome and many spires. Begun about the time the dual mon-archy was formed, this ambitious government building was not completed until 1904.

Once the capital has been left behind, the traveler in Hungary will find few large cities. Debrecen in the east is in the center of Hungary's stock-raising region. The plains country to the west of Debrecen has been irrigated and con-verted to agricultural use as Hungary's breadbasket. Szeged, in the south, lies in a fertile farming district that is noted for the production of paprika. Paprika and Tokay wine, in fact, are Hungary's two most important food exports.

Most of Hungarian life is lived in the rural villages of the rolling countryside and the broad level plains. Many of the primitive prewar mud-brick houses, with their thatched straw roofs, have been replaced in the postwar years by small neat cement dwellings with tiled roofs. The village main street has perhaps been paved, electricity has been installed throughout the village, and the government has established a community center to house both local and itinerant cultural and educational programs.

But the village lanes remain either muddy, rutted with frost, or choked with dust; there is no running water or modern sanitation; and the men of the village still patronize the *csarda* (char'-dah), the local smoke-filled tavern, to drink rough wine and spend long hours in talk.

Church holidays and folk festivals sometimes bring out the traditional village costumes. The young women are especially vivid in their short full skirts, puffed out by a dozen or so starched petticoats, and their stiff lace head-dresses with multicolored ribbons hanging down in back. But most country women go about their everyday chores in drab utilitarian clothing, their heads covered with the deep babushka that is worn by farm women throughout eastern Europe.

Everyday meals in the Hungarian villages are built around breads; homemade noodles and dumplings; thick bean or lentil soups, often with smoked pork or *kolbász* sausage in them; meat stews and cabbage dishes, especially meat-and-rice-stuffed cabbage, *töltött káposzta*, which is cooked with layers of sauerkraut and with spareribs, ham hocks, or sausages for richer flavor.

In late summer peppers and squash are stuffed with ground pork combined with rice or bread and simmered in a rich tomato gravy for *töltött paprika* and *töltött tök*. *Tökfözelék*, the yellow-green Hungarian summer squash, is shredded and cooked with vinegar, dill, and sour cream for a uniquely good vegetable to serve with meats or even by itself. Because the raw squash is often shredded like cabbage and layered with salt to be put away for winter use, Hungarians also call the cooked squash dish *tök káposzta* (squash "cabbage").

Even in the humble farm villages, vegetables are seldom transferred from the boiling pot to the table. The Hungarian housewife prefers to sauce her green beans, cabbage, cauliflower, spinach, or even potatoes with sour cream enhanced with minced fried onion, dill, paprika, buttered bread crumbs, or tiny bits of ham. Often she layers the vegetable with some of these ingredients and makes it in a casserole. Very poor families may make an evening meal of braised shredded cabbage combined with noodle squares, which is eaten with dark homemade bread.

The Hungarian nobility kept vast hunting preserves, and the game tradition lives on in rural Hungary. Pheasant, grouse, partridge, hare, and wild duck from the shores of Lake Balaton and Neusiedler Lake are all popular. Also from Lake Balaton and from the waters of the Danube and Tisza rivers comes the *halászlé*, the fresh-water fish soup or fish stew of Hungary.

Fogas (a tender, delicately flavored white-meat fish with few treacherous bones), sterlet (which is related to sturgeon), perch, pike, trout, and carp are all candidates for the pot. Country people and river fishermen often cook the *halászlé* in a copper kettle over a campfire built close to the shore of the river or stream in which the fish was caught.

Everyday desserts in Hungary are frequently noodle or dumpling dishes, filling enough to top off a one-dish meal such as a goulash soup, a stuffed vegetable, or a fish stew. Hungarian families are very fond of *túrós csusza*, a nonsweet dessert of noodles combined with cottage cheese, sour cream, and crisp-fried bacon. Sweet noodle desserts are prepared with walnuts or poppy seeds, sugar, and cinnamon. Plum or apricot dumplings are wrapped in a mashed-potato dough, cooked in boiling water, and rolled in bread crumbs and sugar.

Fánk (doughnuts) and *aranygaluska* ("golden dumplings"), a large cake of butter-dipped "bubbles" of yeast-raised dough sprinkled with raisins, nuts, and sugar, are Hungarian household specialties. The fancier *torta* and the rich pastries and buttery cookies are reserved for special occasions. Most often they appear in Budapest coffeehouses and pastry shops where, in the old imperial tradition, they are served during the afternoon coffee hour with tea or with coffee topped with whipped cream.

Coffee is rather expensive in Hungary, so tea may be substituted at family meals. Mineral waters are plentiful in Hungary and are frequently the only mealtime beverage. Or a sparkling mineral water will be mixed with wine. Even though Hungary is basically a wine-drinking country, beer is also a very popular beverage.

HUNGARIAN GYPSY LIFE AND FESTIVAL CELEBRATIONS

Gypsy music, alternately gay and frenzied, sad and wailing, sets the mood in Hungary. Gypsy life is seen in the towns and villages, and the gypsy influence permeates Hungarian folk music as well as serious music. The most famous Hungarian folk dance, the *czárdás*, begins in a slow tempo and spins off at a rapid, whirling pace. Hungarian composers like Liszt, Kodály, Dohnányi, and even Bartók used folk tunes or reflect their influence in their major works. Others like Lehár and Kalman wrote music in the Viennese operetta idiom.

Like Hungary's other invaders from the East, the gypsies are believed to have drifted westward from India, but their trek was a slow and unaggressive one with possibly a long stopover in Egypt, from which the word "gypsy" is said to derive. The gypsy tongue, Romany, appears related to the Hindi language of India, and the gypsies' swarthy complexion, dark hair, and dark eyes also seem to link them to India.

Despite their contributions to Hungarian culture, most gypsies prefer to remain with their own people. Almost every town has its gypsy quarter, usually quite run-down, unattractive, and unsanitary. Those gypsies who continue to be itinerant generally work as tinkers, roaming through the countryside mending household utensils. Some work as traveling blacksmiths, migrant farm workers, and many of course are musicians. Like the Jews in Hungary who were almost completely wiped out by Hitlerian edict, the gypsies too were ordered to be annihilated. Many, however, eluded the Nazis through their itinerant habits.

Of all Hungarian festivals, the feast of St. Stephen on August 20 is surely the oldest. In former years it was traditional for peasants to arrive in droves from the surrounding countryside to attend the great procession in Buda honoring Hungary's patron saint, and to remain to celebrate for several days or even a week. St. Stephen's Day calls for rich eating, including foods like chicken paprikash and *gesztenyekrém* (chestnut cream), an opulent dessert of puréed chestnuts, egg yolks, brandy or rum, and whipped cream.

Hungary, with two thirds of its population Catholic, generally regards Christmas Eve as a fast day, and a fish dish, perhaps a fish *paprikás*, is often served at the evening meal. Christmas Day is celebrated with roast chicken or with turkey for those who can afford it. In the villages, one of the family geese that has been waddling around in the muddy lanes comes to the table. New Year's Day dinner means roast suckling pig with a red apple in its mouth and possibly a four-leaf clover in its snout for luck. *Fánk*, the carnival doughnuts, often filled with raspberry jam, make their first appearance at the New Year.

Husvét, as Easter is called in Hungary, translates as "meat-taking" or "the taking of meat" after the long Lenten fast. An Easter dinner features baked ham or roast lamb, a richly creamed vegetable, and possibly a fancy *torta* for dessert.

The feast of St. Mark on April 25 has always been an important day in pastoral Hungary, for the winter wheat is then but eight weeks from harvest. Traditionally, the village priest offered prayers for the safe delivery of the crop against any mishaps such as storm or drought, hail or fire. Even in modern Hungary, with its many collective farms and relatively few private holdings, one cannot overestimate the importance of the grain harvest to the peasant. Although corn and rye are also much-used cereal grains in Hungary, wheat is the true mainstay.

The successful harvesting of the wheat late in June brings on the first of a series of joyous country festivities, to be followed later in the summer by corn husking, grape harvesting, and hog butchering. Meantime Hungarian city folk and townspeople have probably gone off to the shore resorts of Lake Balaton where they can enjoy sandy beaches, bathing in shallow waters, sailboating, and the illusion of a summer by the sea in a country that is miles and miles from the nearest seacoast.

A HUNGARIAN MENU AND SOME HUNGARIAN RECIPES

Gombaleves (Mushroom Soup)	or	*Bableves Csipetkével* (Bean Soup with Pinched Noodles)
	*	
Csirke Paprikás (Chicken Paprikash)	or	*Gulyás* (Goulash)
Galuska (Flour Dumplings)		*Metélt* (Noodles)
Cékla Saláta (Pickled Beet Salad)		*Zöldbab Saláta* (Marinated Green Bean Salad)
	*	
Palacsinta (Dessert Crepes)	or	*Almásrétes* (Apple Strudel)
	Tea (Tea)	

GULYÁS

(*Goulash*)

- 1½ tablespoons lard or other fat
- 2 medium red onions, sliced
- 2 teaspoons sweet paprika
- ½ tablespoon lard or other fat
- 3 pounds trimmed beef rump cut in 1½-inch cubes

 1 clove garlic (optional)
   salt
 1 teaspoon paprika
 1 teaspoon caraway seeds (optional)
 1 8-ounce can tomato sauce plus ½ cup water, *or*
    1½ cups canned tomatoes, cut up, with liquid
 2 green peppers, seeded and cut in long ¼-inch strips
1½ tablespoons flour
 ½ cup sour cream

Melt lard in a large heavy stewpot. Add onions, separated into rings, and cook just until limp, not brown. Add the 2 teaspoons of paprika, blend, and cook a few minutes longer on low heat. Remove onions and set aside. Add additional ½ tablespoon of fat to stewpot. Add beef cubes, one layer at a time, and brown on medium high heat. (Boneless rump of beef is a very good cut to use for this dish.)

As beef browns put garlic through a press, add to meat, and sprinkle all with salt. Return all browned beef and onions to pot. Add paprika, caraway seeds, and tomato mixture. Cover tightly and cook over low heat 1¾ hours or until meat is just tender. Add green pepper strips and cook 15 minutes longer.

In a small bowl combine flour with enough cold water to make a smooth paste. Blend in a few tablespoons of the gravy, return mixture to stewpot, and simmer to thicken. Add sour cream (first thinning it with some of the gravy). Heat through without boiling. Check seasoning. Serve goulash with noodles or boiled potatoes. The garlic and caraway seeds in this recipe are really Austrian and Czech additions. Serves 8 to 10.

CSIRKE PAPRIKÁS

(Chicken Paprikash)

 3 tablespoons lard, butter, or margarine
 2 medium red onions, finely diced
 1 tablespoon sweet paprika

1   tablespoon wine vinegar
1   3½-pound frying chicken, cut in eight pieces
    salt
2   tablespoons flour
1   cup chicken bouillon (2 chicken bouillon cubes dis-
    solved in 1 cup boiling water)
1½ tablespoons flour
¾   cup sour cream

Melt 1 tablespoon of the fat in a large deep skillet that
has a cover. Add onions and sauté until golden and tender,
not brown. Stir in paprika and wine vinegar. Add 1 more
tablespoon of fat. Wash chicken pieces and pat very dry,
then place in skillet, one layer at a time. Sauté on both sides
just until golden and rosy, not browned. Salt chicken while
it is sautéing.

Set chicken pieces aside and add last tablespoon of fat
to skillet. Blend in the 2 tablespoons of flour with a wooden
spoon. Add chicken bouillon gradually and cook, stirring
constantly, until smooth and thickened. Return all chicken
pieces to the pan. Spoon a little of the sauce over them,
cover skillet tightly, and cook on low heat ½ hour. Remove
chicken pieces to a bowl. Blend together in a small bowl the
1½ tablespoons flour and the sour cream. Add a little hot
gravy, return mixture to skillet, cook stirring until thickened. Return chicken pieces to pan, heat through, and serve
with *galuska* or noodles. Serves 4.

GALUSKA

(*Flour Dumplings*)

1⅞ cups sifted all-purpose flour (2 cups less 2 tablespoons)
½   teaspoon salt
2   eggs, beaten
½   cup water
3   tablespoons melted butter or other fat

Sift together flour and salt. Add water to beaten eggs.
Add to flour mixture and beat smooth. Add 1 tablespoon of

the shortening. Have ready 3 quarts of boiling salted water. Drop half-teaspoon mounds of dumpling dough into water. Dough will be soft. To prevent dough from sticking to spoon, dip spoon into the boiling water before adding each dumpling.

Keep water boiling and do not cook too many *galuska* at once. After dumplings rise to the top, let them boil gently for about 5 minutes. Drain and set aside. When all dumplings are cooked, melt the remaining 2 tablespoons of the fat, preferably butter, in a large pot. Add dumplings. Swirl in butter to heat through, and serve with paprikash or other gravy dishes. Serves 4–6.

TÖKFÖZELÉK

(*Squash in Sour Cream*)

1½	pounds yellow summer squash
	salt
1	tablespoon butter
1	medium onion, minced
1	cup water
2	tablespoons cider vinegar
2	tablespoons minced fresh dill
½	cup sour cream
2	teaspoons paprika

Pare squash and shred or grate coarsely into slivers about ½ inch long. Place in a large bowl, salt well, and let stand 10 minutes. Squeeze the water from the squash with your hands to eliminate as much liquid as possible. Melt the butter in a large deep skillet and sauté the minced onion. Add the squash, water, vinegar, and dill. Cover tightly and cook slowly for 40 minutes or until the squash is very tender. Stir in the sour cream and the paprika. Salt to taste. Heat through gently without boiling. Garnish with minced fresh dill or a dusting of paprika. Serves 4 to 5.

PALACSINTA

(*Dessert Crepes*)

2	eggs
½	cup sifted all-purpose flour
¼	teaspoon salt
1½	tablespoons sugar
1	cup milk
1	tablespoon melted butter
	butter for frying
	apricot or other jam
	confectioners' sugar

Beat eggs with a wire whisk in a medium-size bowl. Add flour and beat smooth. Add salt, sugar, milk, and the tablespoon of melted butter. Blend smooth. Choose a frying pan that has an 8-inch cooking surface. A Teflon-coated pan works very well in preparing these crepes. Grease pan with a very small amount of butter. Bring butter to sizzling at medium-high heat. Pour enough batter into pan to coat bottom with a medium-thin layer. Pour any excess back into bowl. Fry until just golden brown. Lift edge to loosen and flip crepe quickly with fingers or with large pancake turner. Fry other side until light golden brown. Transfer to platter, spread with 1 tablespoon jam to within 1 inch of edge. Roll up. Repeat until all crepes are completed, keeping finished crepes warm in a 200-degree oven. Sprinkle with confectioners' sugar and serve. Makes 8 to 9 crepes; serves 3 to 4.

YUGOSLAVIA

I T MAY BE SAID that Hungary's national dish is *gulyás*, Austria's is *Schnitzel*, and Germany's is *Sauerbraten*, but what is the national dish of Yugoslavia?

This question is almost impossible to answer. Yugoslavia, the "land of the south Slavs," is made up of diverse historical and geographical regions that are today organized into six autonomous republics and two autonomous provinces. Yugoslavia speaks three separate languages, uses two different alphabets, worships in three major religious faiths, and eats at least four different basic cuisines.

Unlike other nations with diverse origins, Yugoslavia is not a melting pot. The flavors of her Adriatic seacoast, her verdant Alpine foothills, her Danube River plain, and her almost impenetrable mountains have not fused to produce a national cuisine. Yugoslavia's regionalisms, which are one with her turbulent and divisive history, have been stubbornly preserved for centuries in Yugoslavia's kitchens.

For example, the geographic region of Dalmatia on the Adriatic coast was long under the dominion of the republic of Venice. The Italian influence is strong here, and a fish-and-olive-oil cookery is in evidence. Northwestern Yugoslavia, which includes the autonomous republics of Slovenia

and Croatia, discloses an Austro-Hungarian cuisine—schnitzels, dumplings, and pork-and-sauerkraut dishes—the result of centuries of Austrian imperial rule.

When we reach eastern Yugoslavia and the autonomous republic and ancient kingdom of Serbia, we are in the Balkan world—a Byzantine-influenced land where the religion is Eastern Orthodox and the dishes range from grilled pork kebabs and vegetables stuffed with ground pork and rice to flaky pastries layered with cheese.

Most of central Yugoslavia, the ancient stronghold of the Turks, is a mountainous region spired with minarets, as this is where Islam, in the fourteenth and fifteenth centuries, made the greatest number of converts from Christianity. In the autonomous republic of Bosnia-Hercegovina in this region, the Moslem taboo on pork is reflected in the use of lamb-and-rice stuffings for peppers, squash, onions, tomatoes, and eggplant, and in the use of mutton fat for cooking. The Turkish tradition in Bosnia means sticky-sweet desserts drenched in honey or sugar syrup.

Yugoslavian people are as regional as Yugoslav foods. A man will tell you that he is a Serbian or a Montenegrin, a Croatian or a Slovenian, long before he will clarify matters by explaining that he is really a citizen of Yugoslavia. And indeed Yugoslavia did not come into existence as a nation until 1918, nor was it even called Yugoslavia until 1929.

Yugoslavia shares borders with seven European countries and manages to have a long, island-sprinkled seacoast as well. This seems surprising until one realizes that Yugoslavia is not a small country by European standards. Quite the contrary, she is larger in area than West Germany.

Proximity to Italy and the Adriatic provides western Yugoslavia with a Mediterranean influence in terms of climate as well as cuisine. The weather is mild the year round in Dalmatia, and summers are rain-free. Austria and Hungary on Yugoslavia's northern border give her a taste of the culture of *mittel-Europa* and a continental climate of hot summers, cold snowy winters, and year-round rainfall. Romania, Bulgaria, Greece, and Albania on the east and south are Yugoslavia's Balkan neighbors. The climate here is also con-

tinental, but with extremely hot summers in the southerly regions of Yugoslavia.

Balkan is a Turkish word meaning mountain, for mountains were the most impressive feature the Turks encountered when they first swept into eastern Europe from the plains of Asia.

The Turks reached Yugoslavia in the fourteenth century, before they took Constantinople in 1453. But they were neither the first nor the last of Yugoslavia's numerous invaders and would-be conquerors. In ancient times they were preceded by the Greeks, who were followed by the overpowering Romans.

The western part of Yugoslavia lay so close to the ancient civilizations of the Mediterranean world that it was inevitable that both Greeks and Romans would come to call. Beginning about 500 B.C., the seafaring and colonizing Greeks established settlements along Yugoslavia's Adriatic coast, mingling with the native Celtic and Illyrian peoples of the region.

In the centuries just preceding the birth of Christ, the Romans conquered an area that included a large interior portion of Yugoslavia as well as the coastal region. They named the territory Illyricum. Roman rule meant Roman cultural heritage and a legacy of Roman architecture for

FROM PLUM

BRANDY TO

TURKISH COFFEE

western Yugoslavia. An amphitheater for gladiatorial bouts still stands at Pula, and farther south along the coast, at Split, sprawls the palace of the Emperor Diocletian. Diocletian, who lived from A.D. 245 to 313, was himself an Illyrian, an army officer from the provinces who did so well in the Roman military forces that he rose to become emperor of Rome.

The wines and brandies, fruit juices and sweet preserves for which Yugoslavia is famous may be traced to classical times and to Greco-Roman plantings of grapevines and fruit-bearing trees from the Mediterranean lands. (Olive groves were also established on the Dalmatian coast during the classical era.) Even discerning Romans praised the wines of Illyria in ancient times. But even better known than Yugoslavia's wines, which have only begun to be exported on a large scale since World War II, is Yugoslavia's *šljivovica* (shlyee'-vo-vee-tsa), or slivovitz, a potent, colorless plum brandy.

Plump, juicy blue plums grow exceptionally well in that longitudinal belt of central Yugoslavia where the Mediterranean climate begins to give way to the continental climate. Yugoslavia's plums make a delicious *pekmez* (fruit butter or thick, smooth jam) as well as a rich bottled fruit juice. But it is especially difficult to imagine Yugoslavia without its *rakija* (ra'kee-ya: general term for brandy) which may be distilled from other fruits, but which is most often distilled from the juice of the plentiful plum.

Šljivovica is a way of life in many parts of Yugoslavia. Countless cafés stretching from Belgrade to remote country towns are open as early as 6 A.M. to dispense small glasses of brandy to factory and office workers alike, most of whom begin their seven- or eight-hour day no later than 7 A.M. Often a midmorning bracer is taken at 9 or 10, and from midafternoon when the workday ends to very late evening, the *kafana* is never empty.

This does not mean that there is widespread drunkenness in Yugoslavia. *Rakija* is simply the ritual national stimulant of a people who also nicely balance wines and beers, mineral waters and fruit liqueurs in their beverage intake. In the heavily Moslem reaches of Yugoslavia, natural mineral waters and the sweet, non-alcoholic juices of cherries, apricots, berries, and grapes are preferred to alcoholic beverages which, along with pork, are prohibited to devout followers of Islam.

The fruit-growing heritage of the classical civilizations may also be partly responsible for Yugoslavia's *slatko* (preserved fruit, either whole or in large pieces, in a sweet, crystalline syrup). *Slatko*, which is one of the proudest culinary accomplishments of Serbia's housewives, can be prepared with almost any fresh fruit. It is particularly luscious when made with watermelon rind.

A visit to a Serbian home means a prompt hospitality offering of *slatko* from a handsome glass serving dish. Also on the serving tray is a glass of cold water. Traditionally, the guest helps himself to a small teaspoonful of the sweet and follows it with a refreshing draft of water. Usually this ritual is completed with a small glass of *šljivovica*, tossed down all at once to the Serbian toast *Na zdravlje!* (To health!). And finally, unless the guest is shortly to sit down to a meal, the hostess will produce small cups of thick, sweet, Turkish-style coffee.

The division of the overextended Roman Empire into eastern and western portions in A.D. 395 had a profound effect on the territory that is now Yugoslavia. It lay in the very middle between the Latin world of the western empire, centered in Rome, and the Greek-Byzantine world of the eastern empire with its capital at Constantinople. Thus an imaginary wall arose along a north-south axis in the territory of Yugoslavia, dividing it into two distinct halves.

By the sixth century, when the pagan Slavic peoples began filtering into Yugoslavia from the north and the east, their religious destiny had already been determined. Those who remained in eastern Yugoslavia would subscribe to the Byzantine heritage and would worship in the Eastern Orthodox church. Those Slavs who migrated to western Yugoslavia were to worship in the Roman Catholic faith. This split in Christianity came about as a result of the Byzantine rejection of Roman papal authority. It became final in 1054. A third faith was to be added with the advent of the Turks in Yugoslavia.

While the three languages of Yugoslavia—Serbo-Croat, Slovenian, and Macedonian—are all related Slavic tongues, the alphabets of the East and West are different. Eastern Yugoslavia took the Cyrillic alphabet developed by the Byzantine missionary, St. Cyril, in the ninth century. Cyrillic, which was derived from Greek, is also used in writing Russian and Bulgarian. Western Yugoslavia continued to use the Latin alphabet. Thus Serbo-Croat is a single spoken tongue, but two written languages. Serbian is set down in Cyrillic; Croatian in Latin. Today, in Serbia and other parts of eastern Yugoslavia, school children learn Cyrillic in the first grade and add the study of their language in the Latin alphabet in the third grade.

In Serbia the Slavs settled down to a pastoral existence, organizing themselves into family tribal groups of from ten to one hundred persons. Farming and animal herding were communal activities. The male-dominated and male-descended working and living community was called the *zadruga*. By the fourteenth century Serbia had become a powerful feudal state under the Nemanja family, and it dominated much of Yugoslavia and even reached westward to the Adriatic. Medieval trade routes crisscrossed the Nemanja empire, bringing goods from Constantinople to Venice and picking up for export to both East and West such Serbian trade goods as skins and livestock, honey and wax, and iron ore.

The Turks were not likely to overlook such a prize as the Serbian empire. Bypassing Constantinople for the time, they rushed on to Yugoslavia where at the battle of Kosovo in 1389 they destroyed the Serbian forces.

Now came the increasingly oppressive centuries of Turkish overlordship. Most Serbs refused to become Moslems and were reduced to the status of serfs. The surviving members of the nobility fled in preference to losing their rank and privileges. The Turks imposed forced labor decrees and exacted heavy taxes in both money and goods. These were difficult burdens for the conquered to bear, but harshest of all was the yearly conscription of male children, who were taken by the Turks to far-off Istanbul for lifelong service in the janissary corps.

It was during this period of Serbian history that the colorful and song-praised *hajduk* (hy'-dook), the bandit-hero who took to the hills and waged guerrilla warfare against the Turks, came into existence. Turkish rule was to last for five hundred years in Serbia, well into the late nineteenth century. In Macedonia, in southeast Yugoslavia, the land was not wrested from the Turks until the Balkan Wars of 1912–13.

The Turks penetrated elsewhere in Yugoslavia with varying degrees of success. In Bosnia, in central Yugoslavia, they remained for as long as they did in Serbia, and finding the population there torn between the faiths of Eastern Orthodoxy and Roman Catholicism, they made a large number of converts to Islam. In Dalmatia they met the power of Venice and permitted themselves to be bought off with yearly tributes which the rich little republic, the "queen of the Adriatic," was well able to afford. Slovenia, in the most remote corner of northwest Yugoslavia, was never really ruled by the Turks, although it was often raided. But the fiercest resistance to the Turks came from the Montenegrins, who from their craggy mountain retreats in south central Yugoslavia waged a centuries-long battle against Turkish infiltration.

Turkish foods and dining customs are the inevitable outcome of the Turkish occupation of so much of Yugoslavia. Turkish coffee is drunk throughout the land, and the Serbian hospitality ritual of *slatko* and cold water is almost identical to the Greek ritual, both having been adopted from the Turks. In Serbia, Bosnia, and Macedonia, meals most often begin with a variety of appetizers known as *meze* in Turkish.

Yugoslavian *meze* are usually accompanied by glasses of *rakija* in non-Moslem homes and may consist of mildly ripened white sheep's-milk cheese, of slices of smoked ham, beef, or dry sausage, or of tiny savory hot biscuits prepared with pork cracklings. Another hot appetizer and one that somewhat resembles the Turkish *boerek* is *gibanica* (gheeba-nee-tsa), a layered pie of cheese and flaky, many-leaved Byzantine pastry. The cheese used in *gibanica* is traditionally combined with aged *kajmak*, a fermented dairy product much used in Serbia which is prepared from the skimmed cream of boiled cow's or sheep's milk. Cut in small pieces, *gibanica* makes an excellent *meze*; cut in meal-size portions it makes a fine luncheon or supper dish.

Turkish-style stuffed vegetables ranging from *punjene paprike* (stuffed green peppers) to *sarma* (stuffed rolled cabbage, sauerkraut, or grape leaves) are immensely popular in Serbia and Bosnia, and the spit-grilled meats of these regions are the distinct legacy of the Turkish horsemen and herdsmen.

In Serbia a favorite meat for grilling is boneless pork, served in small chunks directly from the skewer. This dish is called *ražnjići* (razh'-nyee-tchee). A similar dish is *ćevapčići* (tchev-ap'-chee-tchee), tiny "sausages" of fresh finely ground beef, or beef mixed with other meats. Cooked over charcoal at outdoor cafés and in small garden restaurants, these grilled Serbian meats produce an aroma that is certain to entrap the passerby. When the meat used for *ćevapčići* is kneaded into large, flat, circular patties and grilled on both sides like hamburger, the dish is called *pljeskavica* (plyes'-ka-vee-tsa).

A Serbian mixed grill will include *ražnjići*, *ćevapčići*, pork chops and slices of liver, and is always accompanied by a large mound of chopped raw onion (not a mild variety) and tiny, tear-producing hot peppers. In Bosnia and in Macedonia veal is often used in preference to pork, and the most popular grilled meat of all is *šiš-ćevap* (shish′-tchevap), Turkish-style shish kebab prepared with chunks of lamb strung onto skewers with onions, tomatoes, and green peppers.

Soured milk products also show up in Yugoslavian cuisine as a consequence of the Turkish herdsman influence. Cucumber and lettuce salads are dressed with yogurt in Macedonia, meat balls are cooked in a yogurt sauce in Bosnia, and Serbian stuffed vegetables are topped with a tablespoonful of yogurt or sour cream.

Yugoslavian desserts that may be traced to the Turks include *halva*, a very sweet farina pudding; *kadaif*, a shredded-wheat-like pastry; and *baklava*, a flaky, layered pastry. The latter two are stuffed with ground nuts and bathed in a glistening syrup. Surprisingly the Serbs also prepare a pumpkin pie with the flaky Byzantine pastry. The filling, of native-grown pumpkin pulp, milk, and eggs, is not unlike that used in New England pumpkin pie.

In Bosnia a cube of sweet, chewy Turkish delight, coated with sugar and cornstarch and tinged with the flavor of lemon, orange, or rose water, is the inevitable accompaniment to the Turkish coffee that is served as a hospitality gesture the moment guests arrive.

ITALIAN AND AUSTRO-HUNGARIAN INFLUENCES IN YUGOSLAVIAN CUISINE

The narrow coastal region of Dalmatia (a southern arm of Croatia and administratively part of that autonomous republic) combines the flavors of Roman antiquity and the Venetian Renaissance. All up and down the coast and on the offshore islands are tiny walled towns modeled after the largest and most famous of the coastal cities, Dubrovnik. While Venice ruled most of Dalmatia from the thirteenth through the eighteenth centuries, Dubrovnik itself was an independent republic until 1815, a city-state that like Venice

grew wealthy through trade. With its magnificent Adriatic harbor, its Venetian Gothic palaces, and its stone-paved white streets, Dubrovnik has been called "a Venice without canals."

While the towns of the Adriatic coast are bustling with people and are today enjoying a new-found prosperity due principally to the tourist trade, the countryside is very poor. The land is hilly, stony, and infertile, most of its topsoil having been washed away centuries ago. As in many parts of Greece and Italy, the olive tree, the fig tree, and the grapevine grow well, and small crops of other southern fruits can be managed. But meat is relatively scarce and fish is the main source of protein.

The Adriatic Sea provides hundreds of kinds of fish, including mackerel, mullet, bluefish, bonito, sardines, and squid. Many of the smaller fish are fried whole in olive oil. The Dalmatian fish stew called *brodet* combines several varieties of fish along with onions, tomatoes, herbs, and wine for a *bouillabaisse*-like dish that varies up and down the coast and changes from day to day depending on the contents of the net. *Brodet* is usually served over a mound of fluffy rice.

The Dalmatian specialty of smoked raw ham called *pršuta* is quite similar to the northern Italian *prosciutto* and makes an excellent *meze* anywhere in Yugoslavia. Dalmatia is, however, the only region of Yugoslavia where cheese is eaten at the close of the meal in Mediterranean fashion, rather than at the beginning as an appetizer. Aside from cheese, fresh fruit is offered for dessert and also ice cream. There are no special cakes or pastries. Dalmatian wines, many of which are produced on the islands of the Adriatic, are plentiful and are more popular than beer or spirits in this part of Yugoslavia.

Traveling northward and eastward from Dalmatia, one leaves the land of olive oil and enters the domain of lard. Butter, too, is used in cooking throughout northern Yugoslavia. Slovenia, Croatia, and the Vojvodina (Voy'-vo-dee-na: an autonomous province linked to Serbia and lying north of the Danube) are Slav regions that did not become free of the crumbling Austro-Hungarian Empire until 1918.

The countryside grows increasingly level as one travels eastward from the almost Tyrolean villages of Slovenia to the prairie-like Vojvodina. This is good dairy and herding country; pigs and chickens are seen everywhere in the barn-yards, and geese wander in the muddy lanes of the villages. Eastern Croatia and the Vojvodina are one with the Pannonian plain that extends north into Hungary. This is the breadbasket of Yugoslavia and the sector where the government of Marshal Tito found it most practical to establish

large and efficient collective farms. But both here and in the hillier regions of small farms there is still a great deal of private farming, and the trend is away from rather than toward collectivism.

In Slovenia the Austrian influence is at its strongest. Many types of *šnicla* (shnits′-la: schnitzels) are offered on restaurant menus. Soups float hearty dumplings or noodles; sweet noodle dishes and strudels of yeast dough, such as the nut-filled *potica* (po′-tee-tsa), or of flaky pastry pop up for dessert. German-style sausages such as those of the town of Kranj in Slovenia are immensely popular. *Pivo* (beer) is a favorite beverage, although it often shares table honors with spritzers of white wine and soda.

Croatia and the Vojvodina show the Hungarian influence with dishes such as goulash, chicken paprikash, and *palačinke* (pa′-la-chin-ke: the Hungarian *palacsinta*). These delicate dessert crepes, filled with *pekmez* (jam; often apricot or plum) or chocolate, are skillfully prepared in Yugoslavia, even in the south. Rich nutted tortes, often served with extra whipped cream on the side, are offered for dessert at festive meals and at the coffee hour in northern Yugoslavia. But the coffee itself, even in Alpine Slovenia, is *Turska kafa*, thick, dark, and sweet.

Along with the many central European dishes encountered in northern Yugoslavia, one finds the Balkan-tinged foods of Serbia and Bosnia which Yugoslavia shares with Romania, Bulgaria, Greece, and Turkey: *djuveč* (dyoo′-vech), a baked dish of meat and many vegetables that often includes rice and sometimes potatoes as well; and *musaka*, a seasoned ground-meat and tomato mixture layered with eggplant, squash, or potatoes, topped with an egg-and-milk custard, and baked to a delectable crustiness.

A popular soup of Yugoslavia, especially in the north and in Serbia, is *kisela čorba*, literally "sour soup." It is usually thick with meat and vegetables and is made sour through the use of sauerkraut juice or vinegar. Sour cream may be added to mellow the tart flavor. Along the Danube in Yugoslavia the great soup is *alaska čorba* (fisherman's soup) prepared by the river fishermen or *alasi* from their fresh-water catch, which usually includes sheatfish and sterlet, perch and pike. Traditionally the smaller Danubian fish are cooked first, along with herbs and onions, to provide a broth in which the larger fish, cut into filets, are then simmered. This stewlike soup is also made both tart and mellow in flavor through the use of vinegar and beaten egg yolks.

In remote Montenegro, where few foreign influences have penetrated and where the land is extremely mountainous, sheep raising is a principal occupation, yielding a menu of lamb and mutton dishes, sheep's-milk cheeses, yogurt, and *kajmak*. Patches of maize are grown on small mountain farms, and corn meal produces various porridge-like dishes —corn-meal mush combined with cheese, eggs, or *kajmak*. Mountain honey and fruits from small upland orchards provide Montenegrins with simple desserts and sweets.

Oddly enough it was neither the Slovenians nor the Croatians, nor even the Serbs of the Vojvodina, who precipitated the hostilities with the Austro-Hungarian Empire in 1914. Instead it was the Bosnians who, having suffered the Turks for nearly five hundred years, were freed by Russia through the Russo-Turkish War of 1877 and were then promptly handed over to Austria by the victorious Russians.

In 1908 Bosnia's status was amended by Austria from that of an occupied region to an annexed territory. In 1914 Gavrilo Princip, a Bosnian patriot, assassinated the Archduke Franz Ferdinand, heir to the Austrian throne, in Sarajevo, the lovely minareted city that lies in a haze-shrouded bowl deep in the mountains of Bosnia.

Serbia was considered to have instigated this act of violence since she had the best reasons for doing so. Recently emerged from the Turkish yoke herself and anxious to unify the divided south Slavic world, Serbia resented Austria's receiving dominion over the ancient heartland of Bosnia.

World War I righted the wrongs done to the south Slavs, but it did not produce a harmonious Yugoslav nation. Unsuccessful and dictatorial kings and ministers met violent deaths, imprisonments, and banishments in the period between the two wars. But with the close of World War II and the political ascendancy of Marshal Tito the country began

at last to achieve stability. Tito, who had emerged as Yugoslavia's wartime resistance leader against the Nazis, also led
the movement to put down opposing forces within Yugoslavia.

In 1948 Yugoslavia threw off Soviet domination and
broke out of the satellite orbit. Today the most politically
and economically independent of the East European Communist countries, Yugoslavia places the fewest restrictions
on personal freedoms and enjoys good trade relationships
with both the East and the West.

YUGOSLAV MARKET
PLACES, KAFANE
AND SAINTS' DAYS

A most enchanting feature of Yugoslav life is the color and
variety of the country's food markets. Although sleek, modern supermarkets may be found in Slovenia's capital of
Ljubljana, in Belgrade, and even in Titograd, the rebuilt
capital of far-off Montenegro, one need only wander a short
distance from these twentieth-century emporia to find the
outdoor peasant market heaped high with farm produce.
Depending on the region of Yugoslavia one happens to be in,
the vendors may be Slavic farm wives clad in babushka,
full skirts, apron, and stout, mud-soiled boots, or they may
be Moslem men in fezzes or turbans, their women standing
just behind them in semitransparent head shawls and Turkish trousers.

The peasant markets both in towns and small villages
attest to the large amount of private farming that exists in
Yugoslavia. Close by the peasant stalls one also finds, in the
same market place, the permanent stalls of the socialist
sector of the economy. These sell basic foodstuffs produced
on the collective farms. Prices are fixed and perishables are
kept in limited supply to avoid waste.

The peasant market, on the other hand, is the place for
good-natured haggling, where prices rise and fall in keeping
with the laws of demand and supply. Often the housewife
who has arrived too late in the day to buy milk or butter at
the socialist food stalls must turn to the peasant market

where she will pay more now that the daily supply of fixed-price items has run out.

While Belgrade and other cities and towns now boast modern multiple-dwelling housing with all modern facilities, there are still many homes in Yugoslavia without refrigeration. And even the city woman, if her background is rural as is so often the case in Yugoslavia's rapidly changing economy, prefers to shop daily for food in summer and several times a week in winter. The market place is not only the place to hunt for bargains and for the freshest of seasonal foods, but also a social club where gossip is exchanged and where one keeps abreast of the local news.

For men the social gathering place is the *kafana*, the café or coffeehouse. Here one can sit for hours over a *šljivovica* or a cup of Turkish coffee. Some patrons drink beer while others prefer white-wine spritzers. If hunger prompts, one orders *ćevapčići* or salted sheep's milk cheese with chopped raw onion. Many outdoor cafés and garden restaurants open with the advent of warm weather and are patronized by women and by family groups. *Sladoled* (sla'-do-led: ice cream) is a favorite refreshment, as is fresh lemonade or the bottled fruit juices that come in a dozen different flavors.

Since the working day in Yugoslavia usually begins at 7 A.M. and ends by 2 or 2:30 P.M., most families have a large midday meal at about 3. This is followed by a two- or three-hour siesta and then by an evening promenade not unlike the delightful Spanish *paseo*. From about 5 or 6 to 8:30 or 9 P.M. the main streets of Yugoslav towns are thronged with strollers indulging in the daily *korzo*. Shops and stores, many of which close for the siesta hour, remain open during the *korzo*. Once the shops close for the day, the strolling crowds thin, and now the *kafane* begin to fill to capacity.

Yugoslav holidays range from such occasions as May Day, Tito's birthday, and the Day of the Republic (November 29, commemorating the founding of the post-World War II Yugoslav state) to the rites of obscure Moslem sects. Since Yugoslavia is a land where three major world religions are followed, it is not surprising that two Christmases are celebrated—the Roman Catholic on December 25 and the Serbian Orthodox on January 7—as well as a secular New Year on January 1. This last holiday combines the traditional Christmas and New Year festivities with an exchange of greeting cards and presents, decorated trees, and much feasting and revelry.

While Communist party officials may show little interest in traditional religious practices, many Yugoslav families observe the old holidays of their faith. The government does not prevent their doing so. Socialist shops sell religious articles, and the government itself has undertaken the

restoration of the country's monasteries, mosques, and
churches to ensure the preservation of the national culture.
Priests receive pensions and other socialist state benefits.

Among many Yugoslavs of the Serbian Orthodox faith,
the most important religious holiday is the family saint's day
known as the *Krsna Slava* (baptism celebration). This custom derives from the ninth century when the Slavs were
converted to Christianity. The Christian saint on whose day
the family was baptized replaced the pagan deity that the
family had formerly honored. It became the custom for the
family saint's picture to hang in the family home and for
the saint to be carried forward through the male line. A
Serbian Orthodox woman renounces her family saint when
she marries. She takes the saint of her husband's family
unless, of course, she happens to marry a man with the same
family saint. Different families who honor the same saint—
Sveti Jovan (Saint John), for example—all regard themselves as being related to one another.

On the *Slava* a large yellow candle which must burn all
day is lighted beneath the saint's picture. Relatives and
friends are invited to partake of a sumptuous dinner. Often,
if the guests come from afar, the *Slava* may continue for
two to three days. An important food at the *Slava* is the
koljivo or *žito*, a molded "cake" of boiled unmilled wheat

blended with ground walnuts and sugar and decorated with raisins and sweetmeats. The *koljivo*, which must be taken to the church to be blessed after it is prepared, symbolizes life through the use of grain, and the hope for sweetness in life through the use of sugar or honey. It is a dish that goes back to pagan times, just as the *Slava* itself has pre-Christian roots.

A YUGOSLAVIAN MENU AND SOME YUGOSLAVIAN RECIPES

Šljivovica
(Plum Brandy)

Sir   and/or   *Pršuta*   and/or   *Gibanica*
(Cheese)   (Smoked Ham)   (Serbian Cheese-
                                           Filled Pastry)

*

Kisela Čorba
(Sour Soup)

*

Mešano Meso na Žaru   or   *Sarma*
sa Sirovim Lukom   (Stuffed Cabbage Leaves)
(Mixed Grill with
Raw Onions)

Krompir
(Potatoes)

Salata od Paradajza   or   *Zelena Salata sa Kiselim*
(Tomato Salad)   *Mlekom*
                         (Green Salad with Yogurt
                                Dressing)

*

Potica   or   *Voće*
(Slovenian Nut Roll)   (Fresh Fruit)

Turska Kafa
(Turkish-Style Coffee)

GIBANICA

(Serbian Cheese Pie)

1	pound farmer cheese or dry pot cheese
2	eggs, beaten
½	cup sour cream
1	teaspoon salt
⅛	teaspoon white pepper
⅓	cup grated Parmesan cheese
6	tablespoons melted salt butter
½	pound paper-thin pastry sheets (sold in stores as strudel leaves or as Greek *phyllo* pastry)

Add cheese to beaten eggs. Blend well. Add sour cream, salt and pepper, and Parmesan cheese. Brush the bottom and sides of a 9 x 9 x 2-inch baking pan with a little of the melted butter.

Open package of pastry sheets, remove one sheet and keep remainder covered with a damp towel or plastic wrap to prevent drying out. Place pastry sheet, loosely fitted, in bottom of baking pan. (Sheets may be roughly cut to size of pan and trimmings used to make up an additional layer or layers; piecing does not affect baked *gibanica*.)

Using pastry brush, butter first pastry sheet. Place another sheet atop this one, butter it, and continue until there are eight buttered layers in pan. Spoon on one-third of the cheese mixture. Add two more buttered pastry sheets. Spoon on next third of the cheese mixture. Add two more buttered pastry sheets and remainder of cheese mixture. Top with six to eight more buttered pastry sheets, brushing top leaf well with remaining butter.

Bake at 350 degrees for 35 to 40 minutes or until *gibanica* is golden brown and puffed. Cool slightly. Cut in small squares and serve as appetizer, or cut in large squares and serve as main luncheon or supper dish. Serves 6 as main dish.

RAŽNJIĆI

(*Grilled Pork Kebabs*)

1½-inch cubes of well-trimmed boneless pork loin
salt and pepper
chopped raw onion

Place pork cubes on skewers and grill or broil quickly close to heat, turning once. If desired, pork cubes may be alternated on skewers with cubes of veal cut from leg. When meat is done, sprinkle with salt and pepper and serve at once with a mound of chopped onion. Allow 6 to 8 cubes per person.

SARMA

(*Stuffed Cabbage Leaves*)

1	head cabbage, about 3 pounds
2	tablespoons butter, lard, or other fat
1	large onion, diced fine
1¼	pounds ground beef and pork (half each, or two-thirds pork)
6	tablespoons uncooked rice
2	teaspoons salt
⅛	teaspoon pepper
2	tablespoons minced fresh parsley
1	No. 2½ can tomatoes
1½	cups drained sauerkraut (about ½ pound in bulk)
	Additional salt and pepper

Strip 14 to 16 whole outer leaves off cabbage. Cut out and discard thick part of leaves near core. Rinse leaves, place in a pot of boiling water, cover pot, and turn off heat. Let stand in water 15 minutes. Remove leaves and drain.

Melt fat in large deep skillet, add onion, and sauté. Remove skillet from heat, add ground meat, rice, salt, pepper, and parsley. Blend thoroughly.

Grate remainder of head of cabbage (should yield about 4 cups). Place grated cabbage in large saucepan, add tomatoes (with liquid), and cook briskly, covered, for 20 minutes. Add sauerkraut, and salt and pepper to taste. While cabbage mixture is cooking, distribute meat mixture among cabbage leaves, placing a mound on each leaf. Roll up leaves, tucking in ends, and fasten each with a toothpick. Place half of cooked cabbage-sauerkraut mixture in bottom of large deep skillet or heavy stewpot. Add cabbage rolls. Top with rest of mixture. Pour ½ cup water over all. Cover tightly and simmer 1¼ hours.

Remove toothpicks from *sarma*. Serve cabbage rolls with cabbage-sauerkraut mixture and, if desired, top with a spoonful of sour cream or yogurt. Serves 6 to 8.

ZELENA SALATA SA KISELIM MLEKOM

(Green Salad with Yogurt Dressing)

	lettuce or other greens, washed, cut into shreds, and chilled
1	part olive oil or salad oil
3	parts yogurt
	salt
	freshly ground black pepper
	dash sugar
	garlic, put through garlic press (optional)

Combine oil, yogurt, seasonings, and garlic to taste. Beat, pour over greens, toss to coat thoroughly, and serve.

POTICA

(Slovenian Nut Roll)

1	cake yeast or 1 envelope active dry yeast
¼	cup lukewarm water

⅜ cup milk, scalded
¼ pound butter
2 tablespoons sugar
¼ teaspoon salt
1 egg plus 1 egg yolk
2 teaspoons grated lemon rind
2½ cups sifted all-purpose flour

Add yeast to water and dissolve. To scalded milk add butter, sugar, and salt. Remove from heat and stir until butter melts. Beat eggs in a bowl. Add cooled milk-and-butter mixture. Add yeast mixture and lemon rind. Sift into mixture 1½ cups of the flour and beat with a wooden spoon until dough blisters. Add rest of flour. Dough should be stiff enough to knead. Add a little more flour if necessary.

Turn dough out onto floured board or pastry cloth and knead until smooth and satiny. Place in bowl, cover securely, and let rise in a warm place until doubled. Punch down and let rise again until doubled. When dough has doubled for the second time, roll it out to a 12 x 18-inch rectangle, about ¼ inch thick.

Nut Filling

1½ tablespoons butter, melted
1 cup ground walnuts or filberts
½ cup sugar
½ teaspoon cinnamon
1 egg, beaten
1 egg white, beaten stiff
½ cup finely chopped walnuts
¾ cup raisins
  beaten whole egg

Spread rectangle of dough with butter. Combine nuts, sugar, cinnamon, and beaten egg. Blend smooth and fold in beaten egg white. Spread on dough. Sprinkle entire surface with chopped walnuts and with raisins. Roll up tightly. Place on greased jelly roll pan or cooky sheet, curving *potica* slightly so that it will fit. Brush with beaten whole egg.

Cover with plastic wrap or waxed paper and let rise in a warm place until doubled in size. Bake at 350 degrees about 25 minutes or until deep golden brown. Cool thoroughly. To serve, cut crosswise in slices. Makes about 16 servings.

BULGARIA

Bulgaria is an almost legendary land of yogurt and roses; of healthful vegetables, nuts, and grains; and of spry octogenarians whose parents, having just rounded their first hundred years, are very much alive and kicking.

For many years it was believed that yogurt was the secret of the good health and long life enjoyed by the Bulgarian people. Nutritionists have carefully studied the Bulgarian diet, but no startling facts have come to light. It is true that, in addition to yogurt, Bulgarians eat more vegetables and whole grains than other Balkan peoples, and less meat, that nuts appear often in Bulgarian dishes, and that sunflower oil is the most widely used cooking fat as against butter, lard, or mutton fat. Nevertheless, other national groups who eat a similar diet do not attain the phenomenal life spans of the Bulgarians, and so it must be assumed that Bulgarian longevity is also due to a heredity factor.

Bulgaria lies in the southeast corner of Europe and is fringed on the south by parts of Greece and Turkey, which separate it from the Aegean Sea. The country is made up of horizontal ribbons of mountain chains and river valleys. In the north the Danube River basin separates Bulgaria from its northern neighbor, Romania. On the east Bulgaria is

bordered by the Black Sea. Along this 175-mile coastline known as the Dobruja there are fishing villages and ruined Greek temples that date back to the sixth century B.C. Today Bulgaria's Black Sea coast is rapidly developing into an international resort area. With their white beaches, turquoise waters, and modern, high-rise hotels, Varna and other coastal cities are now holiday centers that lure tourists from all over eastern and central Europe.

As elsewhere in the Balkans, the ancient Greek colonists and traders were followed by the Roman legions and lawmakers, and by A.D. 44 Bulgaria was part of the Roman Empire. The Slav herders and farmers reached Bulgaria in the fifth century. In the seventh century the Slavs were overrun by the Bulgars, a nomadic Asian people who brought yogurt to Bulgaria, intermarried with the Slav population, and took the Slavic language.

The merging of these two principal groups produced a strong medieval Bulgarian state that at times challenged the power of the Byzantine Empire at Constantinople. But the fourteenth century spelled doom for the Bulgarian Empire, then at its zenith. Like the Serbian domains to the west, the Bulgarian Empire fell to the Turks.

Turkish rule in Bulgaria grew harsher and more corrupt with the passing centuries. After the Turks had been driven back twice from the gates of Vienna and routed out of Hungary, they intensified their hold over the subject lands nearer home. Opportunistic Greek, Turkish, and Bulgarian merchants exploited the poor, forcing many Bulgarian men to go abroad to earn a livelihood, while the women and children who remained behind provided a cheap labor market. Ignorance and intense poverty were widespread.

A series of unsuccessful Bulgarian uprisings against the Turks in the nineteenth century gave Russia the excuse she had been seeking to crush Turkey. As a result of the Russo-Turkish War of 1877, Bulgaria gained a measure of independence and was eventually able to break free entirely from Turkish domination. Her ordeal under the Turks had lasted five centuries.

The Turks left a strange heritage in Bulgaria. Despite

five hundred years of bloodletting, they are perhaps best represented in contemporary Bulgaria by the miles and miles of Damask roses which they planted in that country beginning in the 1600s. Exquisitely fragrant, these vast plantations of lovely red and white blooms with oil-rich petals provide the attar of roses highly prized in perfume making. In the rose-growing valleys and in the rose-oil distillery towns, this strange gift of the Turks is today termed "Bulgaria's gold."

When Elie Metchnikoff, the Russian biologist, visited Bulgaria toward the end of the nineteenth century, he grew curious about the cold white soup that was eaten by peasants everywhere throughout the country. This soup was *tarator*, a mixture of chopped cucumbers, ground walnuts, garlic, olive or sunflower oil, and the tangy soured milk called *kiselo mleko* or *leban*—popularly known as yogurt. The origin of this soup was Turkish, for like the early Bulgars, the Turks too made extensive use of soured milk.

BULGARIAN MEALS: YOGURT SOUP TO ROSE-WATER DESSERTS

Metchnikoff was struck by the good health and the seemingly delayed aging processes among the Bulgarian people. Not only did the peasants eat *tarator* for lunch and for supper, but they spooned yogurt onto their porridges of whole grain cereals, they used it as a sauce with fish and meats, they combined it with fruit or drizzled honey on it and ate it for dessert. They combined yogurt with milk, eggs, and cheese and baked it into a firm pudding which was eaten either hot or cold. And most of all they ate yogurt all by itself.

While the best grade of yogurt is said to come from sheep's milk, it may also be prepared from the milk of cows, goats, or buffaloes. The preparation is simple. Each day a small amount of the yogurt on hand is added to the supply of fresh milk. This "starter" sours the new milk which in turn provides starter for the next batch of fresh milk. The Bulgarian peasant's reason for souring milk is the age-old one of preservation. Fresh milk simply does not keep very well without refrigeration.

Metchnikoff's interest in yogurt led to his identifying the lactic acid bacteria that gives yogurt its characteristic tart, refreshing flavor and custardlike consistency. He named it *Lactobacillus bulgaricus* after the Bulgarian people. While this bacillus is one of the many bacteria beneficial to man, and while yogurt is certainly a nourishing food, claims for its value as a unique health provider and life extender have perhaps been overenthusiastic. Nor is yogurt, which is prepared from milk containing part or all of its butterfat, a particularly effective food for the low-calorie diet.

While *tarator* is a yogurt-base soup that makes a very good chilled meal starter in warm weather, other Bulgarian soups with poultry, meat, or vegetable bases, and which are eaten hot, also include yogurt. Such a soup is known in Bulgaria as a *chorba*. It is tangy and slightly creamy, and may include rice and chopped mint added to a lamb-broth or chicken-broth base. A *chorba* is not very different from the *avgolemono* soup of Greece which is made both tangy and mellow through the use of lemon juice and beaten eggs. In

fact, Bulgarian cuisine is probably closer to that of Greece than to any other Balkan cuisine. The Austro-Hungarian influence did not reach as far east as Bulgaria, and the Byzantine-Turkish heritage is very strong.

Meals begin with *meze* in Bulgaria as they do in Turkey. Very popular is *masline*, an appetizer spread of mashed black olives blended with oil and lemon juice. Also well liked is *zelen haiver* ("green caviar") which is not caviar at all, but rather another mashed spread, this one of roasted eggplant and green pepper seasoned with garlic and fresh parsley. Cheeses are served as appetizers in Bulgaria—both the white uncured varieties and the yellow *kashkaval*, a more strongly flavored type that is produced throughout the Balkans. *Pasterma*, a spicy dry sausage of Turkish origin, is cut in very thin slices and also served as a *meze*.

Nearly ninety per cent of Bulgaria's population belongs to the Eastern Orthodox religion (Moslems make up the next largest group) so there are few restrictions regarding alcoholic beverages. Therefore most Bulgarian meals begin with a glass of *slivovitza* (plum brandy) or of *mastika* (grape brandy flavored with aniseed and with the resinous sap of the mastic tree). These are drunk from small glasses and are taken with *meze*. Bulgaria also produces, as part of its Greek and Roman heritage, both red and white wines, and has a great many natural mineral waters.

The Black Sea and the Danube provide the Bulgarian menu with a variety of fish. However, the mountainous rural regions that make up much of Bulgaria do not receive shipments of fish from the sea and rivers and so must depend on the catch of local mountain streams. Whatever the catch, a popular dish in Bulgaria is a fish *musaka*, layers of fileted fish in a tomato-and-onion sauce alternating with layers of sliced fried eggplant. Like the better known meat *musaka* of the Balkans and Turkey, which is usually prepared with ground lamb, this version too is topped with an egg-and-milk custard and is then baked crisp and golden. Another Bulgarian fish dish that shows the Turkish influence is baked carp or other large whole fish stuffed with a nut filling that includes fried onion, raisins, and chopped nuts. Many varieties of nuts—filberts, almonds, hazelnuts, and particularly walnuts—grow abundantly in Bulgaria.

Meat dishes tend to be smothered in, or at least thickly surrounded by, vegetables in Bulgarian cuisine: *musaki*; *dolmi* (stuffed squash, peppers, cucumbers, and other vegetables); the rolled-up *dolmi* known as *sarma* (stuffed cabbage or grapevine leaves); *jachnia* (a stewlike dish of one vegetable plus many onions cooked with a small quantity of meat, or sometimes no meat at all); and the well-known *guivetch* prepared with a great variety of vegetables and often, but not always, lamb.

The *guivetch* takes its name from the earthenware casserole in which it is baked. *Guivetch* is best in summer when it can be made with as many as ten or more fresh vegetables, which blend and intermingle to produce subtle new flavors during the long, slow cooking process.

In winter dried beans and lentils, root vegetables, and pickled fruits and vegetables, along with grains and yogurt, are the mainstay of the Bulgarian peasant diet. No summer produce is ever wasted. Anything that can be preserved by pickling goes into the barrel of brine or is steeped in vinegar and spices.

Rice (*oriz*) is prepared in Turkish pilaf style, being first lightly sautéed in fat and then cooked in just enough stock to be completely absorbed and to tenderize the grains. Onions, garlic, and stinging red peppers are used with a free hand in Bulgaria, both in cooking and in garnishing foods. Potatoes are less popular here than in other Danube countries, but bread as elsewhere in the Danube world comes in thick, heavy-crusted loaves and is of the nourishing whole-grain variety.

Bulgarian desserts, as might be expected, are distinctly Turkish. There is the *halva* pudding of farina or rice flour, well sweetened and flavored with orange-flower or rose water, as well as the *halva* confection of crushed sesame seeds, sugar, and oil. A Turkish rice pudding prepared with pulverized rice, milk, sugar, and rose water is a favorite dessert in Bulgaria. Whole grains of rice seldom appear in Turkish or Bulgarian dessert puddings. Grains, when uncrushed, are considered to be in the cereal category and are therefore not delicate enough to qualify as a sweet in the luxurious Eastern tradition. *Baklava* and other honeyed pastries filled with crushed nuts, cinnamon, and sugar are principally pastry-shop specialties. Simple Bulgarian meals close with fresh fruit such as *dinya* (watermelon) or with yogurt.

Aside from its role in perfumery, the rose has a number of culinary uses. The excellent Bulgarian rose water acts as a flavoring essence in teas, vinegars, and honeys, in fruit dishes, puddings, jellies, and confections. While a very good jam can be made from rose hips, the berrylike fruit or seed receptacle of the rose plant, the Bulgarian specialty is a jelly prepared with rose petals, cooked with sugar and water and flavored with lemon.

Late in May, in the famous Valley of the Roses in central Bulgaria, the rose workers begin their annual harvesting of rose petals. The roses to be used for oil distillation are picked just before the petals open wide. The rose gatherers, most of them women, begin their work in the fields in the predawn hours of each day, as the blooms are considered to produce the most attar if picked before sunup.

ROSE GATHERING AND WEDDING DANCES IN TODAY'S BULGARIA

This most fragrant of all harvest activities continues well into the month of June, and all the while the rose fields and the rose stills bathe the countryside in the most intoxicating of aromas. Since several hundred pounds of rose petals are required to produce just one ounce of the precious rose attar, this ingredient is used in only the more costly perfumes, lotions, soaps, and other cosmetics.

Cotton and tobacco, olives, and a number of fruit crops, particularly grapes and melons, are grown in southern Bulgaria. Each brings its own harvest and the related activities of tobacco processing, oil pressing, wine making, and the like. Since Bulgaria is under a Communist regime and follows an economic policy very close to that of the Soviet Union, most farms are collectivized. Some private farms

exist, but these are usually in the most mountainous and infertile regions of the country. They are limited in acreage, not only by the rugged terrain, but by government regulation, and often find difficulty in competing with the collective farms in selling their produce.

Despite the government's attempt at streamlining Bulgaria's agricultural economy and replacing the mud village houses with trim brick dwellings, there are still many reminders of the somnolent Turkish era in rural Bulgaria. In front of the shabby village cafés, elderly men with bronzed, deeply seamed faces and hawklike profiles sit about all day languidly puffing tobacco smoke. Many, in their turbans or sheepskin caps and their baggy full-seated trousers, appear to be living relics of the Turkish centuries.

Folk dancing and handicrafts, still practiced in today's Bulgaria, also take one back to former times. Colorful handmade pottery, carved woodenware, and homespun fabrics are engaging examples of the rich Bulgarian craft tradition.

And traveling folk dance groups are as much a part of today's Bulgarian culture as were the itinerant gypsies of former days.

A harvest festival, a wedding, or other special occasion joins villagers, guests, and all comers in the *horo*, the national Bulgarian circle dance in which participants are linked by crossed arms, often holding on to one another by the belt. There are many variations in the steps, patterns, and tempi of the *horo*. The circle may break to form an intricately weaving chain, as directed by the leader of the dance. The music may be supplied by a peasant band of simple homemade instruments—reed pipes, drums, and bagpipes— or by an accordion, an assortment of fiddles, or in the absence of all of these simply by handclapping. If the occasion is a wedding, red wine will flow abundantly, whole young sheep will be roasted, and as each male guest departs he will whisper a bit of advice into the groom's ear and slip a small purse of money into the groom's hand.

Sofia, Bulgaria's capital, is typical of many other parts of Bulgaria in that it is a mixture of the old and the new that has not quite blended. High-rise apartment and office blocks, stark monolithic government buildings, wide boulevards with fountains and neatly planted rose gardens all point to a bustling city of the future. But Sofia does not bustle. Its broad streets are remarkably empty of traffic, for the automobile still has a long way to go to become a mass consumer item in Bulgaria. And in the midst of all that is sleek and new in the city, there still sit the gently crumbling mosques of the Turkish-Moslem world. Sofia seems to be a city poised, not unpleasingly, between the past and the future.

A BULGARIAN MENU AND SOME BULGARIAN RECIPES

Mastika
(Brandy)

Masline
(Mashed Olive Spread)

Zelen Haiver
(Green Eggplant "Caviar")

*

Tarator
(Chilled Cucumber and Yogurt Soup)

*

Guivetch
(Baked Lamb and Vegetables)

Oriz
(Rice Pilaf)

*

Oriz "Pudding"
(Pulverized Rice Pudding
with Rose Water)

or

Kiselo Mleko
(Yogurt)

or

Dinya
(Watermelon)

Kafe Tursko
(Turkish-Style Coffee)

ZELEN HAIVER

(*Green Eggplant "Caviar"*)

1 large eggplant or 2 small eggplants (totaling 1½ pounds)
1 tablespoon olive oil
1 small clove garlic

  1   tablespoon finely cut fresh parsley
  1   medium green pepper, seeded and cut in very small dice
  1   very small "hot" pickled green pepper, cut fine
        (optional)
 ¼   teaspoon salt
        freshly ground black pepper
  1   tablespoon wine vinegar
  1   tablespoon olive oil

Roast whole eggplant in a 375-degree oven for 45 minutes or until soft. Skin. Place in non-metal bowl and mash with a wooden spoon. Heat 1 tablespoon oil in a small skillet. Put garlic clove through a press and add to oil with parsley and green pepper. Cover and cook 3 to 5 minutes, just until pepper loses its crispness. Add to eggplant along with pickled pepper, salt, black pepper, vinegar, and remaining tablespoon of olive oil. Adjust seasonings to taste. Cool and chill. Serve pressed into a shallow dish as an appetizer. Makes 1½ cups.

TARATOR

(Chilled Cucumber and Yogurt Soup)

 1½   cups diced cucumber (1 large cucumber)
  1   teaspoon salt
  1   large clove garlic
 ⅔   cup ground walnuts
  1   teaspoon salt
  2   cups yogurt
 1½   cups water
  2   tablespoons olive oil

To prepare cucumber, pare and slice lengthwise into slender shafts about ¼ inch in diameter. Slice shafts crosswise into thin slices. Add 1 teaspoon salt and refrigerate 1 hour. Put garlic clove through a press and mash in a bowl with walnuts and remaining teaspoon of salt. Blend in yogurt and water. Add cucumber along with liquid that has accumulated. Add olive oil. Adjust salt to taste. Serve chilled. Serves 4 to 5.

GUIVETCH

(Baked Lamb and Vegetables)

1	tablespoon oil
4 to 5	pounds lamb shoulder in large chunks, or four meaty lamb shanks weighing about five pounds
	salt
	freshly ground black pepper
2	onions, diced fine
3	tomatoes, skinned and cut in medium chunks
2	tablespoons minced fresh parsley
¾	cup water
½	pound string beans, trimmed and split lengthwise
2	green peppers, seeded and cut in large chunks
3 to 4	small zucchini (about one pound), trimmed and scrubbed but not pared, cut in 1½-inch chunks
1	one-pound eggplant, pared and cut in 1½-inch chunks
1	tablespoon lemon juice
	yogurt

Heat oil in deep, heavy stewpot. Add lamb one layer at a time and brown well on all sides, sprinkling meat with salt and pepper as it browns. Layer onion, tomatoes, and parsley with browned meat, add more salt and pepper, and add water. Cover pot very tightly and simmer on low heat 1¼ hours.

While lamb is cooking, prepare vegetables. At end of simmering period, transfer lamb to a large covered roaster or oven casserole. Arrange string beans, green pepper, zucchini, and eggplant around and atop meat. Spoon all remaining contents of stewpot over meat and vegetables. Sprinkle with salt and pepper and with lemon juice. Cover and bake 1 hour at 350 degrees.

If lamb shanks are used, remove meat from bones just before serving (it will fall away very easily), discard bones, and return meat in large chunks to *guivetch*. Serve, in baking utensil if possible, along with *oriz* and small individual bowls of yogurt on the side. Serves 8 to 10.

ORIZ

(*Rice Pilaf*)

> 4 tablespoons butter or margarine
> 2 small cloves garlic
> 2 small onions, minced
> 1¼ cups rice, converted long-grain
> 2½ cups chicken bouillon (3 to 4 chicken bouillon cubes
>   to 2½ cups boiling water)
>   salt to taste

Melt butter in large deep saucepan. Put garlic cloves through press and add to saucepan with onions. Cook until onions are limp and yellowed. Add rice and cook, stirring, until rice has yellowed. Add chicken bouillon, cover tightly, and cook over very low heat about 20 to 25 minutes, or until rice is tender and liquid absorbed. Add salt to taste. Serve with *guivetch* and other stews. Serves 6.

ORIZ "PUDDING"

(*Pulverized Rice Pudding with Rose Water*)

> 2 cups boiling water
> ¼ cup rice (not converted type)
> 1½ cups milk
> ⅓ cup sugar
> 1 tablespoon cornstarch
> ½ cup milk
>   rose water or cinnamon, to taste

In Bulgaria and in Turkey this dessert is prepared with uncooked rice that has been pulverized by pounding it in a mortar with a pestle. If using whole grains of rice, prepare as follows.

Add rice to boiling water in saucepan and boil uncovered 15 to 20 minutes, or until rice is soft. (Water should be almost entirely absorbed.) Put rice and remaining water through a coarse strainer or sieve. If it is difficult to force all of the rice mixture through, mash balance left in strainer and then blend it with the sieved rice. Return all rice to saucepan and gradually add the 1½ cups milk and the sugar. Blend smooth, bring to a simmer, and cook, stirring frequently, for about 20 minutes or until mixture has thickened.

Blend the cornstarch with the remaining ½ cup milk. Add to rice mixture. Cook, stirring, about 10 minutes or until thick and glossy. Add a few drops of rose water to achieve a delicate flavor. Add more sugar if desired. Cool pudding in saucepan about 15 minutes, then turn into individual serving dishes. If using cinnamon instead of rose water, sprinkle individual servings with cinnamon. Cool and chill. Serves 4 to 6.

ROMANIA

T HE DANUBE comes to the end of its 1,700-mile journey
in Romania. In this comparatively small country at the
eastern edge of Europe there is room for tall, densely for-
ested mountains, a flat, well-farmed river plain, a sparkling
white-sand seacoast, extensive oil fields, and the shadowy
wildlife world of the 2,000-square-mile Danube delta.

Romanians are as many-faceted as the country in which
they live. Their classical Greek and Dacian-Roman heritage
has been enriched by Slavs and Bulgars, Hungarians and
gypsies, Turks, Austrians, Germans, and Frenchmen. Contemporary Romanian culture reaches back in history to the
days of the Emperor Trajan, and has dipped clear across
Europe to France.

The gifts of the ancient Romans, who settled among the
Dacian tribes of Romania and administered them from A.D.
106 to 271, included a Romance language, a wine-drinking
tradition, and an affinity with the Latin spirit that bred a
yearning for contacts with other Latin peoples of Europe.
Thus Bucharest, Romania's capital, has long been known
as "the Paris of the Balkans," for this city is not only physi-

235

cally modeled after Paris, but has attempted to cultivate the spirit of that city. Strolling the boulevards, frequenting cafés, admiring the city's handsome women, enjoying the pleasures of wine, food, and witty conversation are (ideally, at any rate) considered to be the Bucharest way of life.

After the demise of the Roman Empire, the province of Dacia came under a succession of foreign overlords. During the early Middle Ages, Romania was part of the Bulgarian Empire. Later in that period the independent Romanian feudal states of Walachia (in the south) and Moldavia (in the northeast) emerged, while the region of Transylvania, in the northwest, fell to Magyar rule.

In the sixteenth century the Turks gained control of most of Romania. With Russian help, Walachia and Moldavia eventually threw off the Turks and in 1859 united to establish the independent country of Romania. However Transylvania, the remaining third of the country, had in the meantime merely exchanged one master for another. Its Magyar rulers were succeeded by Turkish rulers, and its Turkish rulers by those of the Austrian Empire, (which in its final stage became the Austro-Hungarian Empire). It was not until after World War I that Transylvania, after a wait of one thousand years, was at last reunited with the mother country.

Under the dictator Antonescu, Romania entered World War II on the side of Nazi Germany, but later withdrew and re-entered on the side of the Allies. The end of the war saw the establishment of a Communist government in Romania. But despite many political controls and a scarcity of consumer goods, the gay international spirit of the Romanians is once again asserting itself, and the country conforms less rigidly to the Soviet line than do several other satellite nations.

In view of Romania's checkered history, it is not surprising that a Romanian meal should begin with Turkish *meze*, continue with a sour Russian-style soup, go on to a Magyar-inspired mixed grill accompanied by an American Indian corn-meal dish, and conclude with either French dessert pancakes or an Austrian chocolate torte!

Despite the welter of foreign influences, Romania does have a distinct national cuisine. The Danube River and the rich world of the delta provide many varieties of fish and above all caviar, the highly prized roe of the sturgeon and of related fish.

At the delta, the river, mighty and swollen, splays out into three great arms that meander toward the waters of the Black Sea. Shaped like a triangle, the entire delta area is a water-webbed world with many floating islands, great reedy marshes, and vine-tangled forests. It is a silent world but for the calls of nesting or migrating birds, and the sound of mink, otter, wild boar, or wildcat crackling through the underbrush.

The arms of the Danube delta are identified as the Chilia, the Sulina, and the Sfintul Georghe. Immense sturgeon are caught in the Sfintul Georghe, and throughout the delta region are fishing villages, fishery stations, and canneries for the processing of bream and carp, sheatfish and pike, all of which seem to grow to excessive size in the organically enriched delta waters.

While not many Romanian dinners are likely to begin with caviar and champagne, a great many do begin with *icre*, a fish-roe paste (prepared from the salted roe of pike, carp, or other fish, seasoned with onion and lemon juice), and with *tzuica*, the strong Romanian brandy distilled from plums.

Other Romanian *meze* are marinated fish, spreads of mashed eggplant or of olives, or a tasty mixture of local sheep's- or goat's-milk cheese similar to the Liptauer spread of Czechoslovakia, Hungary, and Austria. Fish roe is often breaded and fried and served as a first course at dinner. Spitted grilled carp and a regional fish *borsch* are specialties that originated in the delta region. The latter is a rich soup, almost a stew, prepared with several kinds of fish and often with the heads of the prized white beluga sturgeon.

The best known Romanian soup is the *ciorba* (chor'-ba), a sour soup, often containing meat balls or giblets, which is thought to be related to the Russian sour soups. Indeed many Romanian soups and stews go by the name of *bors* which is similar to the Russian *borsch*. Unlike the tangy Greek and Bulgarian soups which are flavored with lemon, a traditional Romanian *ciorba* is flavored with the juice of fermented grains, for lemons are relatively scarce in Romania. In Russia this sour-grain extract is known as *kvass*.

Since grain fermentation is a tedious process, Romanian cooks use many substitutes. Among these are the sour juice of tart or unripe fruits or berries, the juice of sorrel (sour grass) leaves, and very often sauerkraut juice. Yogurt or sour cream is the mellowing agent for the soup or stew.

While Turkish-Balkan main dishes like *ghiveciu* (the Bulgarian *guivetch*), *musaca*, *dolmas*, and *sarmales* are all to be found on the Romanian menu, grilled meats are the real national specialty. *Mititei* are to Romania what *ćevapčići* and *ražnjići* are to Serbia. Like the Yugoslav meats, *mititei* are grilled over charcoal and are to be had at cafés and informal restaurants, or may purchased fragrant and sizzling from vendors who cook them on the spot in the streets of Bucharest.

Mititei are prepared with ground beef that is vigorously seasoned with garlic and well scented with herbs. The meat is molded into tiny sausage shapes for broiling. In fact the word *mititei* means "very small." Traditional accompaniments are tiny hot peppers. For a more elaborate dish the Romanians serve the *gratar amestecat* (mixed grill) of *mititei*, broiled pork chop, broiled liver, kidney, and often other variety meats. Grilled beefsteaks, well rubbed with garlic, are also popular. Both these specialties are usually served planked—that is, on the wooden platter on which they were broiled—and are garnished with fried potatoes and accompanied by cold raw sauerkraut, dill pickles, and the inevitable red and green peppers. The place to go for a variety of choice broiled meats in Bucharest and other Romanian cities is the *zahana* or grill room restaurant. Native red or white dry wines are served in these restaurants. Romanian broilings are of course derived from Magyar and other Asian nomad dishes, but they are stamped with the spicy, zesty flavor of Romanian cuisine, and imbued with garlic in the unmistakable Latin tradition.

Schnitzels, which show the Austrian influence, are prepared with lamb or veal in Romania, while the *tocana* and other goulash-like stews are the result of proximity to Hungary. The region of Transylvania has the greatest proportion of Austro-Hungarian dishes because it was allied to one or both of these countries for the better part of ten centuries.

Game birds from the Danube delta such as wild duck or quail sometimes appear on the Romanian menu. But the delta region is too valuable as a feathered wildlife sanctuary to be raided for the dinner table. The delta's bird population changes with the seasons and the several hundred species that may be observed there range from Arctic geese and Siberian whooping swans to rosy flamingos from the Nile.

Domesticated poultry, however, is always a favorite in Romania. Goose and duck are popular, and chicken is prepared in a variety of ways—braised in a *tocana* with a rich gravy, stewed in a tangy *bors* of sauerkraut juice and sour cream, or cooked in Mediterranean fashion with black olives and white wine.

When maize, the cereal grain of the American Indian, was first brought back to Europe by the Spanish conquerors in the 1500s, it quickly became popular in Spain and Portugal. The Italians took up the growing of Indian corn, and cooked corn meal or corn-meal mush grew to be a staple in Italy where it is known as *polenta*. Although corn was soon being grown throughout the Balkans and eastern Europe, it was received with special enthusiasm by the Romanians. The reason is uncertain. Perhaps once again the Romanians were emulating their Latin cousins in western Europe.

Romanian corn-meal mush or porridge is known as *mamaliga* and is the basis for a great many dishes in Romanian cuisine. It may be eaten for breakfast, lunch, or supper, drizzled with butter, sour cream, or yogurt; it may be garnished with eggs, cottage cheese, or salted fish; or it may be served as an accompaniment to gravied meat dishes. If molded while still hot and then allowed to cool, the *mamaliga* becomes firm enough to slice. It can then be fried crisp and golden in fat, or layered in a casserole with butter and *brinza* (cheese) and baked.

In addition to *mamaliga*, starch accompaniments to meat dishes that appear on the Romanian menu are *cartofi* (potatoes), *fasole* (beans), and *orez* (rice, which is grown on the Danube marshlands). Dried-bean dishes are served extensively as a main course during Lent. They are usually eaten with sauerkraut. At other times the beans, either whole or puréed, are served with well-seasoned Romanian sausages.

When it comes to desserts, summer and autumn offer excellent fresh fruits in season. Many of these fruits—especially cherries, plums, berries, and apricots—are preserved in a sugar syrup for year-round use as *dulceata*, the sweet jams and marmalades that are part of the Turkish-inspired hospitality gesture. As in the Balkan lands of Yugoslavia and Greece, the refreshment offering of *dulceata* and ice-cold water is generally followed by brandy (*tzuica* in Romania) and soon after by cups of Turkish coffee.

Most Romanian desserts are rather international in flavor. The *palacsinta* or French-inspired dessert crepes of Hungary are of course very popular in Romania, where they are known as *clatite*. In emulation of the French *crêpes Suzette*, the Romanians like to sauce their crepes with liqueur or rum and flame them. But *clatite* are also served folded or rolled up around jam or cottage cheese as in Hungary and Yugoslavia.

Flaky, thin Turkish-Byzantine pastry appears two ways in Romania. It is presented as strudel, as in the countries to the west, or as one of the *baklava*-like confections of the Near East. Syrup-drenched *aluat cu nuci* (nut pastries) are a typical Turkish-style Romanian dessert or coffee-hour sweet. But should one want to turn and face westward once again, Romanian cooks and bakers produce light crisp doughnuts, deep-fried fruit dumplings, and creamy nutted tortes that rival those of Vienna.

Unlike their Latin counterparts in western Europe, the Romanians seem to find the continental breakfast too limited to suit their early morning appetites. In addition to dark bread with honey or jam, a Romanian breakfast may include boiled eggs, cottage cheese, and ham or sausage.

Midday dinner is usually eaten between 1 and 2 and is the principal meal of the day for those families whose members are able to return home for lunch. In summer, which is very hot in Bucharest since the city lies neither in the mountains nor at the shore, a siesta period is observed between about 2:30 and 5:30. The evening meal is not served until 8 or later, but there is a great deal of in-between eating done at cafés and street stands in towns and cities. Yogurt, ice cream, Turkish coffee, beer, *tzuica*, and wine (usually combined with soda) are enjoyed at café tables, while Romanian street crowds love to nibble on raisins or on the fresh cherries sold in paper cornucopias on street corners while the season lasts.

ROMANIA'S YEAR-
ROUND FESTIVITIES

In many respects Romania is a year-round holiday resort. Autumn does not mean the end of the vacation season but rather the beginning of the winter sports season in the Carpathian highlands and the Transylvanian Alps that lie to the north of Bucharest. Mountains, densely wooded or capped by fantastic rock formations, make up much of the north central region of Romania. By November the first snows have fallen and the ski slopes at the resorts of Sinaia, Predeal, and Braşov (Brashov) are ready for use.

About halfway between Bucharest and the resort centers of the Transylvanian Alps lies the prosperous oil town of Ploeşti. Here in the mountain foothills there are forests too. But these are forests of steel. Their trees are the oil derricks that have brought renewed industrial growth to Romania in the postwar years.

While many Romanian citizens and workers, as well as visitors to the country, are enjoying brisk winter holidays in the mountains, the peasants are making ready for the New Year. Most Romanians are of the Eastern Orthodox faith, but all faiths—Roman Catholic, Protestant, Moslem, Jewish—are permitted church attendance. A popular New Year custom, probably of pagan origin, is known as the *plugu-şorul*. Country children dressed in deep fur caps, sheepskin jackets, and boots make their way through the snowy village streets pulling the *pluguşor*, a small decorated plow modeled after the great wooden buffalo-drawn plows of the Romanian farmers. The plow symbolizes successful planting and bountiful crops, and as it passes each village house good wishes are extended for health and prosperity in the coming year.

The arrival of spring brings Easter and its Easter Eve Resurrection ceremony as practiced in the Romanian Orthodox Church. This ceremony, with its midnight candle-lighting parade, is followed by an Easter morn meal (eaten just after midnight) of a creamy sour soup prepared with a sheep's head and with lamb variety meats.

A folk festival of Transylvania that takes place each year in May is the *Simbra Oilor*, which combines the events of "sheep counting" and of country feasting and merrymaking. It is on this occasion that the villagers' sheep, having been previously rounded up, depart with their shepherds for the higher mountain pastures where they will graze and fatten during the summer months. The sheep of each villager are milked on the morning of the festival and an estimate is made, from the amount of milk obtained, as to how much cheese will be owed to the sheep owner through the summer.

But sheep milking and cheese estimating are only an aspect of this festival. Dressed in regional costumes of white skirts, or full, wide trousers banded in red and black, the villagers and shepherds bring to the village meadow quantities of their best food and drink. Not until dusk has descended do the weary celebrants return to their homes.

Full summer brings dozens of local fairs and folk festivals

to the mountains, valleys, and coastal regions. Most renowned is the Young Girls' Fair held in July on Mt. Gaina in Romania's western mountains. This fair is a song and dance festival at which one is sure to witness the lively *hora*, the traditional Romanian circle dance performed by both men and women. Especially exciting are the Romanian men's dances of which the vigorous *caluşari*, with its soaring leaps and frenzied rhythms, is probably the most spectacular.

The Young Girls' Fair is also a market fair for the sale of numerous wares, especially Romania's noted craft products which include hand-woven textiles and carpets, exquisite embroideries, ceramics, and carved woodenware. The name of this fair indicates another of its purposes—that of presenting the marriageable girls of the countryside to prospective suitors. It is in reality a coming-out party for the girls of Romania's remote mountain villages.

July and August are also the months for trips through the Danube delta, and for seaside camping and hotel stays at Mamaia and other Black Sea resorts. Constantza is an ancient Black Sea port and also an archaeological site that attracts many summer visitors. Spas for the treatment of numerous ailments abound in Romania, and especially interesting are Romania's famed geriatrics clinics that appear to have made amazing strides not only in lengthening human life span but in slowing down disagreeable aging processes.

August 23 is the Romanian national holiday which marks the beginning of the people's revolution in 1944. September sees harvest festivals throughout the country. In Bucharest and in the towns it is the beginning of the *must* or grape juice season. At every corner appear *mustarii*, little wooden street stands selling the unfermented juice of the ripe newly harvested grapes. Delicious accompaniments to *must*, also sold by the street vendors, are hot *mamaliga* and spicy smoked *pastrama*, traditionally prepared with goat meat.

The markets blaze with the colors of ripe fruits and vegetables in autumn, and of course no village fair is complete without its quota of gypsies. The music and dancing of this exotic people are so vital a part of Romanian life that they have been transmitted to the concert medium through the compositions of the famous Romanian composer and musician Georges Enesco.

As with most of eastern Europe's gypsy population, the old customs survive despite the government's efforts to educate the young and to train them for participation in the national economy. Still a common sight in Romania are the itinerant family or tribal groups of gypsy entertainers—little girls still in their kindergarten years doing the sinuous dances of their people, gypsy women adorned in necklaces of allegedly venomous snakes, and the gypsy man leading on a leash, with a brass ring through its nose, a good-humored performing bear from the Carpathian Mountains.

A ROMANIAN MENU AND SOME ROMANIAN RECIPES

Tzuica
(Plum Brandy)

Icre
(Fish Roe Paste)

*

Ciorba de Perişoare Cu Carne
(Sour Soup with Meat Balls)

*

Mititei	or	*Tocana de Pui*
(Grilled Beef "Sausages")		(Chicken Stew)

Cartofi Prajiti or *Fasole Cu Unt de Lemn* or *Mamaliga*
(Fried Potatoes) (Beans with Olive Oil) (Corn-Meal Mush)

Salata Verde	or	*Varza Acra*
(Green Salad)		(Sauerkraut)

*

Aluat Cu Nuci	and/or	*Fructe Crude*
(Nut Pastries)		(Fresh Fruit)

Cafea
(Coffee, Turkish Style)

CIORBA DE PERIŞOARE CU CARNE

(Sour Soup with Meat Balls)

3	cups beef bouillon
1	onion, diced
1	carrot, pared and sliced in thin strips
2	ribs celery with leafy tops, crosscut in very thin slices
½	cup sauerkraut juice
1	tablespoon finely cut fresh parsley
1	tablespoon finely cut fresh dill
1½	tablespoons rice
1	egg yolk
¼	cup sour cream

Add onion, carrot, and celery to beef bouillon (bouillon may be prepared with 3 beef bouillon cubes dissolved in 3 cups boiling water). Cook 20 minutes or until vegetables are tender. Add sauerkraut juice, parsley, and dill. Simmer 10 minutes more. Strain soup, add rice and cook 10 minutes.

Meat Balls

½	pound ground veal (or veal and pork combination)
1	slice white bread, soaked in water and squeezed dry
1	egg white, beaten foamy with fork
½	teaspoon salt
	dash pepper
2	teaspoons finely cut fresh parsley

Combine ground meat, soaked bread which has been crumbled, egg white, salt, pepper, and parsley. Shape into 1-inch balls and add to boiling soup, a few at a time. (Soup should be boiling as meat balls are added.) Cook meat balls 15 to 20 minutes.

In a bowl combine egg yolk and sour cream. Add a little of the hot soup, beating mixture smooth. Return mixture to soup pot and cook a few minutes more. Adjust seasoning. Serve soup and meat balls sprinkled with chopped fresh dill or parsley. Serves 4.

MITITEI

(Grilled Beef "Sausages")

    2   pounds ground beef (preferably neck and tenderloin)
    2   large cloves garlic, put through garlic press
 1½   teaspoons salt
    ⅛   teaspoon freshly ground black pepper
    ½   teaspoon dried thyme
    ¾   teaspoon ground allspice
    ⅛   teaspoon ground nutmeg
    ¾   teaspoon baking soda
    ⅔   cup concentrated beef stock (1 beef bouillon cube
            dissolved in ⅔ cup boiling water)

Combine all ingredients in order given, adding the beef stock gradually. Shape into "sausages" about 1 inch thick and 3 inches long. Allow meat to stand at room temperature ½ hour. Grill outdoors over charcoal or place on rack of broiler pan and broil close to heat so that meat browns quickly. Turn once, allowing a few minutes on each side. Serve immediately with sharp red or green peppers, sour dill pickles, pickled beets, or a tangy salad of cucumbers or wilted lettuce. Makes 24 *mititei*. Serves 6.

FASOLE CU UNT DE LEMN

(Beans with Olive Oil)

    1   cup (½ pound) dried white pea beans
    1   medium onion, diced fine
    3   tablespoons olive oil
    1   tablespoon minced fresh parsley
    3   tablespoons tomato paste
 1½   teaspoons salt
    ⅛   teaspoon pepper
    1   tablespoon flour
    ½   cup cooled bean liquid
    1   teaspoon wine vinegar

Soak beans overnight in water to cover. In morning add additional water if necessary to cover and cook, covered, 1½ hours or until beans are tender. Drain, reserving ½ cup of bean liquid.

Fry onion in olive oil until golden and tender. Add parsley, tomato paste, salt, and pepper. In a bowl blend a little of the bean liquid with the flour; add remaining bean liquid and vinegar. Add to onion mixture and cook, stirring, a few minutes until mixture has thickened. Add beans, heat through, and serve as a side dish with meats or stews. *Fasole cu unt de lemn* may also be combined with fried sausage and served as a main dish. Serves 4 to 6. The *fasole* is also very good chilled and served as an hors d'oeuvre.

MAMALIGA CU BRINZA

(Corn-Meal Mush with Cheese)

3   cups water
1   cup yellow corn meal
1   teaspoon salt
1   cup cold water
3   tablespoons butter or margarine
1¾   cups grated cheese (Romanian *cascaval*, or a
      combination of Swiss and Parmesan)

Bring the 3 cups of water to a boil. Combine the corn meal and salt with the 1 cup of cold water. Add to boiling water, stirring constantly. Cover and cook over low heat, stirring frequently, until thick, about 10 to 15 minutes. Turn corn-meal mush into a 5 x 9-inch loaf pan and let it cool thoroughly.

Run a thin knife along edges and unmold. Cut into ⅜-inch-thick slices. Butter a 1½- to 2-quart baking dish. Place a layer of *mamaliga* slices on bottom. Dot with some of the butter and sprinkle with some of the cheese. Repeat until all ingredients have been used, dotting top layer with butter and sprinkling with cheese. Bake in covered dish at

375 degrees for 20 minutes. Serve with sauerkraut or a tangy salad. Serves 6.

ALUAT CU NUCI

(*Nut Pastries*)

6	tablespoons sweet butter
⅓	cup sugar
2	tablespoons grated lemon rind
¼ to ⅓	pound paper-thin pastry sheets (sold in stores as strudel leaves or as Greek *phyllo* pastry)

Nut Filling

1	cup ground or *very* finely chopped walnuts
⅓	cup sugar
½	teaspoon cinnamon
⅛	teaspoon ground allspice
⅓	cup raisins

Melt the butter and with a pastry brush lightly butter an 8 x 8 x 2- or 9 x 9 x 2-inch baking pan. Combine the ⅓ cup sugar with the 2 tablespoons of lemon rind. Line the bottom of the baking pan with one sheet of the pastry, cut roughly to size. Keep rest of pastry sheets covered with a damp towel or plastic wrap to prevent drying out. Brush sheet in pan with a little melted butter and sprinkle with some of the sugar-and-lemon-rind mixture. Cover with another layer, brush with butter and sprinkle with mixture. Continue until there are five or six layers in the pan. Trimmings can be used to make up some of the layers. This will not affect baked pastry. Combine ingredients for nut filling. Spoon over pastry in pan and then add five or six more layers, using up pastry leaves. Each leaf should be brushed with butter and sprinkled with sugar and lemon-rind mixture. Top leaf should be brushed with butter. Score pastry with sharp knife into 20 rectangles, cutting about ½ inch deep. Pour remaining butter atop and into cuts.

Bake at 350 degrees 20 to 25 minutes or until golden brown. Cut through scorings to bottom. Pour on hot syrup. Serve cool. Makes 20 pieces.

Syrup

⅓	cup sugar
3	tablespoons honey
1	teaspoon lemon juice
¾	cup water

Combine and boil 3 minutes.

RUSSIA

T HE LAND of *borsch* and *blini*, of czars and cossacks, and of the world's first Communist revolution, is also a Danube land. Of course the Danube River touches on a very small portion of the world's largest country, which is officially known as the Union of Soviet Socialist Republics (U.S.S.R.).

This immense land stretches from the Baltic Sea to the Pacific Ocean. The distance from the Polish border to the Bering Strait (across which lies Alaska) is over 6,000 miles, twice the distance from California to New York. It takes ten days to cross the Soviet Union by train; only five days to cross the United States by train. As the Russian people are fond of saying, "Russia is not a country; she is a world."

Flowing northward through Romania, the Danube joins the Prut River at the city of Galati in eastern Romania. Up to that point the Prut has served as the border between Romania and the Soviet Union. From Galati eastward, through the delta region and into the Black Sea, the Prut and the Danube are one. Thus the Danube flows past Russia, the eighth and final country to contribute to the internationality of this great stream.

The terms Russia and U.S.S.R. or Union of Soviet Socialist

255

Republics (often shortened to Soviet Union) are apt to be confusing. Before the revolution of 1917, Russia was the name of that giant land of Caucasoid and Mongoloid peoples—Slavs such as Russians and Ukrainians; Asians such as Uzbeks, Kazakhs, and Siberian Yakuts. There were numerous national groups in Mother Russia, each with its own language, background, and customs.

Since 1922 Russia has been organized into socialist republics of which there are presently fifteen. The range of the cuisines of these republics is truly international in scope. For example, the republics of the Caucasus Mountains are peopled by Armenians and Georgians who eat a Near Eastern cuisine of lamb and rice, yogurt, mint, and stuffed grape leaves. The people of central Asia still drink *kumiss* (fermented mare's milk) and eat horsemeat as did their nomadic ancestors. In the Baltic republics of Esthonia, Lithuania, and Latvia, in the northwest, the diet is Scandinavian, while that of the Far Eastern peoples of the Soviet Union follows the northern Oriental culinary pattern and consists mainly of rice and noodles and boiled or pickled root vegetables.

The historic heartland of old Russia consists of the western part of the Russian Soviet Federated Socialist Republic (known today as the RSFSR or Great Russia), the Ukrainian Soviet Socialist Republic (popularly known as the Ukraine or Little Russia), and the Byelorussian Soviet Socialist Republic (also called Belorussia or White Russia).

These westerly and most archetypal regions of old Russia lie in the European plains region. The land consists mainly of flat or very gently rolling steppes with extremely fertile black soil. In the north the steppes give way to forest lands. Here, in European Russia, in the cities of Novgorod, Kiev, and Moscow, Russian civilization was born. Here the czars came to power and established a feudal state that was to survive into the twentieth century. Here the Russian arts—the music of Tchaikovsky, the plays of Chekhov, the novels of Tolstoy and Dostoevsky, the Bolshoi Ballet, and the Moscow Art Theater—all came to flower. And here the culinary influences of half a dozen cultures flourished and fused to produce one great cuisine.

The early tribes of Russia were nomadic horsemen of Asian stock. The Scythians, who are believed to have been of Persian ancestry, wandered over the steppes of western Russia as early as the ninth century B.C. They were known to the Greeks who reached southern Russia by way of the Black Sea and who set up trade with the semiprimitive, warlike horsemen they found on its shores. By the third century B.C. the Scythians had been overrun by the Sarmatians, a similar people believed to have been their kinsmen.

Well into the Christian era, fierce central Asian tribes swarmed across the treeless plains of western Russia, each group enjoying a brief period of domination over its immediate predecessor. It is from this early period of Russian-Asian civilization that Russia's grilled-meat specialty known as *shashlik* derives.

This dish of fileted chunks of meat impaled on a long skewer and roasted over an open fire is of course closely related to the Turkish *shish kebab*. The meat used for *shashlik* is generally lamb or mutton which has been flavored and tenderized by marinating it in an herbed and spiced oil-and-vinegar mixture. In the Caucasus region of southern Russia, between the Black Sea and the Caspian Sea, the lamb for *shashlik* may be marinated in tart pomegranate juice rather than vinegar. Rice is the traditional accompaniment for

FROM THE SCYTHIAN HERDSMEN TO THE BANQUETS OF THE CZARS

shashlik, but in western Russia, where rice is not grown, a *kasha* (cooked cereal) of buckwheat or other grain makes a good substitute.

By the third century A.D., the Slavic peoples of what is now the Polish–Russian border region had penetrated rather deeply into Russia. As they migrated southward they came in contact with one of the last of the central Asian invaders, the Khazars. This group, who later embraced Judaism and who are believed to have been the ancestors of many Russian Jews, dominated the more peaceful Slavs, most of whom worked as slaves in the Khazar empire. The Slavs brought agriculture to the Russian steppes. Through their patient efforts the treeless plains that had known only the sound of pounding hoofs were gradually converted into fields of rye, barley, wheat, and hardy buckwheat, the grain that is almost synonymous with Russia.

Throughout Russian history, buckwheat *kasha* prepared from the triangular-shaped edible seed of the buckwheat plant was to be the staple of the poor. When cooked with water, milk, or broth, and seasoned to taste, whole buckwheat or coarsely ground groats make a hearty and nourishing porridge. To produce crunchiness and a nutty flavor, the buckwheat grains are often browned before they are cooked with the liquid. A *kasha*, of course, need not be prepared with buckwheat. Other grains such as cracked wheat, rice, barley, and millet are used in the various regions of the Soviet Union.

Buckwheat is not necessarily the grain of the poor, nor is *kasha* the dish solely of the hungry masses. The Russian aristocracy enjoyed a luncheon dish of baked *kasha* and mushrooms brimming with thick cream and topped with generous dabs of melting butter. And one of the most elegant of Russian desserts is *Guriev kasha*. This dish is usually prepared from a milk-rich farina pudding crammed with chopped candied fruits, raisins, and ground nuts. The skilled chefs of the Russian aristocracy prepared this dish in layers, alternating small quantities of the *kasha* mixture with half a dozen skins of clotted cream. The latter were produced by slowly heating very rich milk until a creamy skin formed on top and then transferring the skins, one by one, to a baking dish atop a layer of *kasha*. This procedure required infinite patience. The *Guriev kasha* was then baked until the top skin turned a satiny golden brown. It was presented at table warm and garnished with a border of freshly baked, elaborately executed puff pastry as a further display of the chef's skills.

Like most ostentatious dishes, *Guriev kasha* has a poor man's counterpart which is simply a sweet farina or semolina pudding, with or without chopped fruits and nuts, sprinkled with cinnamon and sugar and browned in the oven.

When buckwheat is ground into flour it becomes an important baking ingredient and is often blended with wheat or other flours. The famous Russian pancakes known as *blini* are prepared from a yeast-raised batter that traditionally includes buckwheat flour. Unlike American flapjacks, *blini* are not served for breakfast. Nor, like French crepes and Hungarian *palacsinta*, do *blini* appear at dessert. They are served principally as a first course at dinner or as a main course at luncheon or supper.

Russians eat their *blini* slathered with melted butter and topped with salted fish and thick sour cream. The fish may be pickled herring, smoked salmon, or whitefish. Very often it is the red caviar that is prepared from salmon roe. A Russian *blini* lover—and what Russian is not—can put away nearly a dozen well-dressed *blini* at a sitting and then go on to the rest of the meal. Some diners prefer to fold or roll the pancake after it has been topped with caviar and sour cream; others eat the pancake flat. *Blini* are eaten one at a time, not stacked like American hotcakes. Appetizer *blini* tend to be three inches or less in diameter, while the main course variety may be somewhat larger.

Similar in name, but otherwise quite different, are the twice-fried Russian *blinchiki*. These are thin, crepelike pancakes fried on one side only, topped with a cheese, fruit, meat or other filling, neatly rolled or folded up, and fried again or baked crisp and golden brown in the oven. *Blinchiki* are served as a main course or a dessert, often topped with

sour cream. They are of course the ancestor of the Jewish *blintz* brought to the United States by Jews from the Ukraine, where this food is very popular. Unlike *blini, blinchiki* crepes are prepared from ordinary white flour and are not yeast-raised.

The agriculturally oriented Slavs also provided Russia with her early vegetable crops. Root vegetables such as potatoes, beets, turnips, carrots, and onions became the traditional ingredients of Russian soups. Along with cabbage, these vegetables could be stored through the long winter months when the ground froze and snow covered the fields.

Borsch and *shchi* (also spelled *stchee* and *s'chee*) are the most popular Russian soups since they do not require a meat base, may be prepared with inexpensive vegetable staples, and when accompanied by bread or a buckwheat porridge provide hot, filling meals throughout the cold Russian winter.

Shchi is principally a cabbage soup, although other vegetables are often included. In summer when it is prepared with fresh cabbage it is known as "lazy" *shchi*. In winter, when sauerkraut is the main ingredient, it is called sour *shchi*. Boiled beef, sausage, or smoked pork often appear in *shchi*, providing a meat and vegetable meal all in one dish. Meat stews, however, such as the Hungarian *gulyás*, are not traditional in Russian cuisine.

In poor peasant homes all across the face of Russia, *shchi* and similar soups were eaten from a common pot. Each member of the family dipped in with a hand-carved wooden spoon. A thick slice of coarse Russian bread was held beneath the spoon to catch the drippings before they ran past one's chin.

Borsch, which is thought of chiefly as a hot beet soup that has a cold counterpart for summer meals, also comes in a multivegetable version that includes cabbage, tomatoes, dried beans, and meat. Such a *borsch* is often of the Ukrainian type. It is usually topped with sour cream and is indeed a meal in itself. Although Russian pumpernickel is traditional with *borsch* and other soups, more interesting accompaniments are *piroshki*, individual pastries of fairly rich dough that are filled with ground meat, *kasha*, chopped cabbage, hard-cooked eggs and mushrooms, or other savory centers. *Piroshki* (plural for *pirojok*) are generally about three inches long and are boat- or finger-shaped. A large version of the *pirojok*, known as the *pirog*, is frequently served at Russian family meals.

The *pirog* is an immense, envelope-shaped turnover containing one or more varieties of filling, each in a separate section. It is cut into portions at the table so that family members and guests may each receive a favorite part of the *pirog* to eat with a beet *borsch* or clear soup. *Vatroushki*, another well-liked soup accompaniment that go especially well with *shchi*, are small open-topped pastries, rather like tiny tarts, filled with a mixture of sieved pot cheese.

Despite the brevity of its summers as compared with its long icy winters, Russia has a number of chilled soups in addition to the well-known cold beet *borsch*. Among these is sorrel soup, prepared from the green-bladed plant known as sorrel or sourgrass. Thickened with beaten eggs and

topped with sour cream, this tart, refreshing soup is beloved by Jews of Russian origin to whom it is known as *schav*. Chilled fruit soups similar to those of Scandinavia and Germany are also well liked in Russia. More characteristically Russian is *okroshka*, a summer vegetable soup of minced or sliced cucumbers, dill, scallions, hard-cooked eggs and, often, leftover meat or fish.

Traditionally *okroshka* is made sour through the use of *kvass*, the home-brewed Russian beer prepared by the peasants from fermented black bread or directly from cereal grains. Well chilled and mixed or topped with sour cream, *okroshka* is to Russia what *gazpacho* is to Spain, a liquid salad. It is perfectly suited to the extremes of heat that Russia's continental climate inflicts in summer.

Summer vegetables are a special treat in Russia. Cucumbers are among the first to appear and are eaten raw or as a cooked vegetable braised in butter with minced onion. Although unknown in Russia until after the discovery of America, corn is now a great favorite in the Ukraine where it grows abundantly and is eaten American fashion, on the cob and dripping with butter. (Turkeys, also of American origin, are raised in the Ukraine.) In summer the Ukraine provides large crops of tomatoes, eggplants, green peppers, and squash.

Following the old Russian upper-class tradition of keeping a *datcha*, a summer house in the country, many Soviet citizens today maintain a country cottage to which they repair on weekends and during vacations from May through August. A small vegetable garden, some fruit trees and berry bushes provide the longed-for diet of fresh vegetables and fruits. In addition there is the opportunity to gather wild honey, to pick mushrooms for drying and wild berries for preserving, and to buy fresh dairy and poultry products from the neighboring farms. The Soviet *datcha* is often a very primitive dwelling without running water or electricity, but it provides a welcome change from the stifling, overcrowded Moscow or Leningrad apartment from which there is little escape through the long winter.

The Slavs of early Russia did not confine their activities

to herding and agriculture. While those of the south toiled for the Khazar overlords, the Slavs of northern Russia established a prosperous trading city at Novgorod. In A.D. 862 they called on the Scandinavian leader Rurik to provide protection against the continuing threat of the Khazars.

With his Viking merchant-warriors known as the Varangians, Rurik established the first stable Russian state and founded a dynasty that was to rule Russia for more than 600 years. It is possible that the very name Russia derives from Rurik and his tribe, who were also known as the Rus. The early period of the Viking-Slav merger saw in 882 the capitulation to the Varangians of Khazar-dominated Kiev (today the capital of the Ukrainian S.S.R.).

Kiev lay close to the world of the Byzantine Empire, with its capital, Constantinople, on the south shore of the Black Sea. Thus the new Russian state absorbed many of the influences of Byzantium, including Eastern Orthodoxy, which became the state religion in 989. From this branch of Christianity emerged the Russian Orthodox Church.

The Scandinavians not only gave Russia her start as a mighty empire, they also gave her *zakuski*, the appetizer foods that resemble those of Sweden's *smörgåsbord* and that give both reason and encouragement to the drinking of

numerous small glasses of vodka. In imperial Russia, dinner parties were often delayed for hours while the guests partook of twenty-five or so different *zakuski*: herring in a variety of picklings and sauces, caviar, smoked fish, shellfish, meats including sausages and *pâtés*, marinated vegetables, and the mayonnaise-dressed meat-and-vegetable salad known as salad Olivier after the French chef of Nicholas II, last of the Russian czars. *Zakuski* are traditionally set out, each variety in its own dish, along with small squares of dark bread and curls of fresh sweet butter. Hot dishes such as mushrooms in cream, meat balls, and chicken livers in wine sauce also appear on the *zakuski* table and are served from casserole dishes.

The memoirs of members of the Russian aristocracy tell of fabulous twelve-course dinners preceded by a *zakuski* table groaning with seventy or eighty varieties of hors d'oeuvres and a score of different types of vodka. Family meals were more modest, beginning with from six to ten *zakuski* accompanied by a carafe or two of potent hundred-proof vodka. The Soviet leaders of modern Russia occasionally ape the vanished aristocracy, but on many state occasions they have found it more practical to present an entire lavish buffet supper of *zakuski* accompanied by vodka and followed by dessert and coffee.

Vodka, an unaged alcoholic liquor distilled from grain, is the spirit most beloved by the Russians. Its very name, which means "little water," implies adoration. Most vodka is colorless, but there are other types as well; a yellowish vodka called *zubrovka* after the grassy herb with which it is flavored; a red vodka so colored by the berries of the mountain ash and known as *riabinovka*; a strong peppered vodka called *peretsovka*; and other strengths and varieties. Since vodka is drunk from tiny glasses and is usually taken with bits of thirst-inducing herring or other highly seasoned food, it is not surprising that most Russians can down ten or more glasses in fairly rapid succession before a meal. And of course with each glass that is drunk the Russians jovially offer the traditional toast, *Vasheh zdorovyeh!* (Your health!).

Although the Rurik dynasty successfully subdued the

Khazars in the ninth century, Russia had not seen the last of the central Asian invaders, for in the thirteenth century the Tartars swept out of the East. Under Batu Khan, grandson of the terrible Genghis Khan, the Mongol tribes known as the Golden Horde set up a huge empire centered near the present Russian city of Volgograd (previously Stalingrad). The Kievan princes were thoroughly subjugated and forced to pay tribute to the Tartar rulers.

The Golden Horde was so named because of the opulence of the camp of the great Batu. But like most Asian barbarians, the Tartars practiced no agriculture, drank fermented mare's milk, and ate raw flesh. Quite unintentionally they introduced new foods to Russia and to other parts of Europe as well: steak Tartar, which was to develop into hamburger, and sauerkraut, adapted from that of the Chinese. They also set the taste for sour milk and sour cream (the Russian *smetana*) which were to be used so extensively in Russian as well as other eastern European cuisines.

The Tartar empire survived in Russia until the fifteenth century. Then its power was challenged by the growing city-state of Muscovy ruled by Ivan III (the Great), grand duke of Moscow. Having refused to pay tribute to the Tartar lords any longer, the Moscovites now proceeded to expand their holdings under Ivan's grandson Ivan IV, known as the Terrible, who was crowned czar in 1547.

In 1613 the Romanov czars came to power and ruled Russia until the Bolshevik Revolution of 1917. The Romanov dynasty gave rise to a succession of Peters and Catherines, Nicholases and Alexanders, some of them "Great" and nearly all of them "terrible" in that they did little to mitigate the harsh excesses of the Russian feudal system. While the peasants endured indescribable wretchedness as serfs owned by their masters and bound to the soil, the ruling classes led lives of indolence and extravagance. In the nineteenth century most of Europe stepped briskly into the age of industrialization, but Russia lagged shamefully behind and was justly dubbed by her European neighbors "the sleeping bear."

The banquets of the early czars were crude affairs, distinguished chiefly by the vast quantities of food consumed, the variety of game and fish, of *kashi* and *pirogi* brought to table, and the totally inebriated state of dinner guests by the time the evening drew to a close. The garnishing and seasoning of food and the refinements of table service were given little attention. There was no special order in which the various dishes were presented or eaten, and desserts were a rarity. Mead (an alcoholic drink fermented from honey) and *kvass* were the principal beverages. Wines were almost unknown, for most of Russia was unsuited to the cultivation of the vine.

The age of Catherine the Great, who ruled Russia from 1762 to 1796, saw the introduction of French influences at the Russian court. Although herself a German princess before taking the throne of Russia, Catherine imported her chefs from France and deeply appreciated many aspects of French culture. Catherine's Parisian chefs introduced sauces rich with eggs, sweet cream, and wine to Russia and brought delicately flavored puréed cream soups to the imperial table. It is interesting to note that the Russian infatuation with all things French suffered a temporary reversal in the early nineteenth century with Napoleon's invasion of Russia. A large segment of the nobility gave up French manners, speech, and dress after 1812 and went thoroughly "native" even to the point of banishing French cuisine and bringing instead dishes like the lowly peasant soup *shchi* to their tables.

Czar Alexander II's Edict of Emancipation of 1861 was designed to "free" the twenty-two million serfs who made up
one third of Russia's population. Through the provisions of
this idealistic and unworkable document (issued as the
opening guns of the American Civil War sounded) it was
hoped that the serfs would be able to achieve land owner-
ship and that the growing unrest of Russia's masses would
be curbed.

Alexander's well-meant reforms could never have been
realized under the conditions of Russia's backward economy,
and the Bolshevik Revolution of 1917 was the inevitable
result of the massive discontent and hopeless inequalities of
the old Russian system.

Russia has made enormous strides under the Communist
regime. In the forty-year period from 1917 to 1957 the
Soviets went from "sleeping bear" to satellite launcher (Sput-
nik I), and achieved still another space feat in 1961 when
cosmonaut Yuri A. Gagarin became the first man to orbit
the earth. On the ground too there have been spectacular
changes. Agricultural production has been streamlined
through the development of the *kolkhozy* (cooperative
farms) and *sovkhozy* (state farms); illiteracy has been almost completely wiped out; industrial production is second
only to that of the United States; and basic necessities like
an adequate diet and warm clothing are available to all. The
starvation that afflicted and even took the lives of many
peasants during the centuries of czarist gorging and glut-
tony is at last only a cruel memory.

The Soviet system has many shortcomings, particularly
when viewed by the citizens of countries that were designed
from infancy along democratic principles. The Soviet Union
can be justly viewed only in terms of Russia's own very
recent medieval past.

Despite the many changes in the Russian way of life since
the revolution, Russians remain hearty eaters, immensely

FOUR MEALS A DAY IN OLD AND NEW RUSSIA

hospitable, and addicted to long hours of talk around the table, particularly at the last meal of the day, a venerable institution known as *vechernyi chai* (evening tea).

Tea drinking in Russia derives of course from China. The pleasantest meal of the day in old Russia was the gathering of family and intimate friends around the samovar, the tall urn with a spigot near its base that was used to boil water for tea. The tea itself was brewed in a small china pot. Charcoal was the traditional fuel used to heat the samovar, and the water was kept bubbling throughout the evening repast which generally began at about ten and often lasted until midnight. The word "samovar" combines the Russian words *samo* (self) and *varit* (to boil) and literally means "self-boiler."

The foods served at evening tea ranged from cold meats, cheeses, and bread and butter to sweet cakes and jam. Tea was served in tall heavy glasses, although the ladies often

drank from their own beautifully decorated personal tea-cups. Preserves of whole strawberries, cherries, or other fruits were often eaten by the spoonful along with the tea, or the jam might be stirred into the tea instead of sugar. Lemon was available in only the most affluent households for it had to be brought from distant regions, but often a slice of apple was put into the tea for its aroma and faint tang.

In Soviet Russia the beloved ritual of *vechernyi chai* still prevails. Although the elaborate table linens and decorated teacups, fancy sweetmeats and formal tea services of the imperial past may be missing, the families of modern Russia still look forward to this daily gathering with its rich rewards of conversation and innumerable cups of steaming tea.

In new Russia, the remaining meals of the day are often hurried affairs eaten at home, at school, or in the factory cafeteria, for most adult members of the family work. The children attend school, and the very young are cared for in the day nursery. Even dinner at five or six o'clock may not be a meal at which the entire family can be present.

Breakfast in Russia consists of tea with milk, slices of either dark or white bread, and usually soft-cooked eggs. Jam is not traditional at breakfast time although the aristocracy was fond of following the continental breakfast custom and often took rolls and jam along with *café au lait* (half coffee and half hot milk).

Zavtrak or lunch was eaten at about one or two o'clock in imperial Russia and although it usually consisted of three or four courses, it was not the main meal of the day. Often it began with a small selection of *zakuski* followed by a hearty soup, a meat or fish course, cakes or pudding, fresh or stewed dried fruit, and tea. Very popular as a luncheon dish was a *pirog* or a similar pastry called a *koulibiak*, a round or rectangular two-crust pie stuffed with layers of fish, onions, and rice, or occasionally with eggs, giblets, mushrooms, and the like.

Sirniki (pot-cheese croquettes), fried in butter and served hot with sour cream, were well liked at luncheon, as were

vareniki (boiled dough pockets filled with cheese or fruit and eaten with melted butter), *blini*, baked *kasha* dishes, and *pashtet* (a well-seasoned baked meat loaf often prepared with liver or game). The close of the meal frequently featured a *kissel*, the Russian national dessert pudding prepared with puréed cranberries, currants, or other tart fruit. These dishes still appear at lunchtime in Russia, but the meal is likely to consist of two courses at most with soups, *kasha*, and cabbage dishes the most common selections. Always popular with the mass of the Russian people is *selianka*, a casserole dish of sauerkraut layered with fish or meat.

Obed or dinner in imperial Russia ranged from an informal family meal to a banquet of sumptuous proportions. At the latter, the *zakuski* was certain to feature caviar of the esteemed beluga type, a salted roe of large, pale gray eggs that comes from the prized white beluga sturgeon found in the Black and Caspian seas. Other types of caviar from the sturgeon and related fish consist of smaller grains and may be gray, black, or red (as from the salmon). A selection of several of the better caviar varieties, served well chilled, was obligatory at imperial Russian banquets, just as it is at Soviet functions today.

A well-flavored bouillon or a delicate purée was the choice for the soup course at a large formal dinner. This was followed by a fish course, a roast course, and a game bird course, plus one or more handsomely garnished vegetable dishes.

There are many typical Russian dishes that may be served at dinners featuring one main course. These include the elegant *Kievski kotleti* (chicken Kiev) prepared from boned chicken breasts that enclose a thick dab of cold sweet butter. The *kotleti* are dipped in a crumb breading, fried in hot butter, and served with a mushroom sauce. The heated butter filling gives the chicken a most delicious flavor but also presents the hazard of spurting butter upon eating. To prevent this the *kotleti* must be pricked with a sharp instrument just before serving.

Distinctly Russian, although it was probably invented by a Frenchman, is beef Stroganoff, strips of fine-quality beef in a mustard-seasoned sour cream sauce. The dish was named for Count Paul Stroganoff, a Russian nobleman of the late nineteenth century, but it was more likely the creation of the count's French chef. Beef Stroganoff is often prepared with tomatoes, mushrooms, and other vegetables, but the purist version includes none of these for the dish was not intended to be a meat stretcher or an economy dish.

Ground meat specialties are popular at Soviet family dinners. *Golubtsi* ("pigeons," or stuffed cabbage) are plump packages of chopped meat and rice wrapped in cabbage leaves, and are said to have originated in the Ukraine. *Kotleti*, the hamburgers of the Russians, are slightly flattened oval or round meat patties served in a sour-cream or mushroom sauce and usually prepared with ground beef and stale bread that has been soaked in water or milk. Smaller versions of these meat cakes are called *kotletki*, while meat balls prepared with similar ingredients are known as *bitki*.

Pojarskiya kotleti are tasty golden-fried chicken croquettes. They are named for Pojarsky, the proprietor of a well-patronized inn at Torzhok on the old carriage road between Moscow and St. Petersburg. Pojarsky used game birds in his famous *kotleti*, but today they are usually prepared with chopped raw chicken or with veal. Still another ground meat specialty of Russia is *luli kebab*, a ground lamb patty that is sometimes grilled on a skewer like *shashlik*.

An elaborate ice cream concoction of French or Italian origin brought most formal Russian dinners to a close. A family dinner in old or new Russia would end with a cranberry *kissel* topped with milk or cream, a sweetened *kasha* or milk pudding, a stewed fruit compote, or fresh strawberries or watermelon in season.

Easter is the high point of the Russian festival year. The date of the Russian Easter is different from that of Easter in the Western Christian countries and follows a solemn Lenten period that lasts for seven weeks. However, Easter is a spring festival in Russia as elsewhere, and its associa-

RUSSIAN FEASTS FROM EASTER TO BUTTER WEEK

tion with rebirth and regeneration seems to have special meaning in a land that has lain for many months under a blanket of frost.

While fewer Russians attend church regularly than in prerevolutionary days, many still make it a habit to attend the Easter Eve service, standing (as is the custom in the Orthodox Church) for several hours during the lengthy ritual. In the old tradition, the darkened church is lighted with hundreds of candles at midnight, signifying the Resurrection. The Lenten fast is broken by a special supper eaten just after midnight. The greeting at this meal is "Christ is risen" and the response is "He is risen indeed."

Most splendid of the Russian Easter foods is the *paskha*, a very rich cheese dessert molded in a tall round or pyramidal shape. Finely sieved cottage cheese, sugar, eggs, thick cream, butter, and chopped dried fruits and nuts are the ingredients of this handsome offering which is always beautifully decorated with candied fruits and other sweetmeats and, if possible, with fresh spring flowers.

In the past most Russian households owned a wooden mold made up of four elongated triangular sections into which the *paskha* mixture was tightly packed. The mold was then inverted over a bowl and the moisture permitted to drain off through a hole at the narrow end for a day or two so that the dessert would be sufficiently firm to retain its shape when unmolded. Lacking this type of mold, the *paskha* was packed into a deep flower pot with a drainage hole at the bottom.

In addition to the *paskha*, it is traditional to serve on this holiday the yeast-raised Russian Easter cake known as *kulich*, which contains raisins and is baked in a tall cylindrical shape with the letters *XV* meaning "Christ is risen" impressed into the top of the cake. The *kulich* is sliced horizontally, never vertically, and the top slice is not eaten but is put back atop the cake each time a slice is removed. The reason for this practice is not entirely clear. The intent may be to keep the cut cake from drying out, but more likely it is to preserve the top slice, with its initials of deep religious significance.

The *kulich* is of course closely related to the Russian *baba* (in Polish, *babka*), a cake that is also baked in a tall round shape and which is supposed to represent a *baba* or matronly woman dressed in a long full skirt. The *baba*, which often appears at *vechernyi chai*, is the most authentically Russian cake and is probably the inspiration for the *baba au rhum* which a French pastry chef may have created by soaking a freshly baked *baba* with a rum-and-sugar syrup.

A slice of *kulich* and a spoonful of *paskha* are served on the same plate and eaten together for dessert on Easter Sunday following an abundant repast which is likely to feature roast suckling pig or roast lamb. Russian crafts include the intricate decoration of wood, metal, pottery, and cloth, so it is not surprising that Easter eggs too receive exquisite patterns and colorings in Russia and are displayed in bowls as an attractive addition to the Easter table.

Soviet holidays figure importantly in Russian life. While only some of the people may celebrate the old Russian Easter, nearly all take part in the May Day celebration which lasts for two days through May 2. This holiday, with its parades and banners, speeches and mass gatherings, was inaugurated as far back as 1889 by the Second Socialist International as a day of celebration for labor. The greatest of Soviet holidays falls on November 7 (lasting through November 8) and commemorates the Bolshevik Revolution of 1917. This event is often referred to as the October Revolution since it took place on October 25 on the old Russian calendar, which was still officially in use at the time.

Christmas takes second place to Easter among Russian religious holidays and its celebration today is often overshadowed by the secular Soviet New Year holiday. Traditional for Christmas Eve among religious Russians is the *kootia*, a honey-sweetened porridge of boiled wheat or rice which in pagan times was intended as a grain offering to the gods to bring good crops in the planting season ahead and a sweet life in the year to come.

As Christmas Eve was an occasion for fasting, the meal usually featured a meatless *borsch* and either fried fish or a fish-filled *pirog*. Christmas Day meant a festive meal of roast poultry stuffed with buckwheat, usually goose in Great Russia and quite often turkey in the Ukraine.

The gayest of the old Russian holidays was *maslyanitsa* or "butter week," the pre-Lenten festival during which all of the fats were supposed to be eaten or otherwise disposed of before the onset of the Lenten fast. *Blini* drowned in *maslo* (butter) were the ideal food for this occasion and it is still customary, even for non-religious Soviet citizens, to eat a dozen or so of these tender buckwheat pancakes at a sitting during butter week. Carnivals and fairs are also part of the traditional celebration of *maslyanitsa* and, because ice and snow still cover most of Russia during this late winter season, the numerous hot buttered *blini* with their toppings of caviar and sour cream are accompanied by many rapidly downed small glasses of vodka.

A RUSSIAN MENU AND SOME RUSSIAN RECIPES

Vodka

Pickled Herring   Red Caviar

*

Borsch
(Beet Soup)

Piroshki
(Savory Filled Pastries)

*

Kotleti (Ground Meat Patties) or Beef Stroganoff or *Kievski Kotleti* (Chicken Kiev)

Buckwheat *Kasha* or Boiled Rice

Sauerkraut or Cucumber Salad

*

Klukveny Kissel
(Cranberry Dessert Pudding)

Chai
(Tea)

BORSCH

(Beet Soup)

5 cups consommé or beef bouillon
1 medium onion, cut in chunks
2 or 3 green cabbage leaves, cut in large pieces
6 peppercorns
4 medium beets
2 tablespoons butter

    1   tablespoon vinegar
    2   tablespoons flour
    ½   cup sour cream

To consommé or beef bouillon add onions, cabbage leaves, and peppercorns, and simmer 45 minutes to 1 hour. Cool and strain. Set broth aside. Pare beets with a potato parer. Grate most of one of the beets on a fine grater. Placed grated beet in a small bowl and mix it with 3 tablespoons water. Set aside.

Cut rest of beet and remaining 3 beets into matchstick strips or thin slices. In a heavy 2-quart pot melt the butter. Add cut beets and stir with wooden spoon until buttery. Add vinegar and ¼ cup broth. Cover pot tightly and simmer beets 30 minutes to 1 hour or until tender. If liquid cooks away add a few tablespoons more of the prepared broth.

Blend flour with some of the cool broth to make a smooth mixture. Add to beet mixture with remaining broth. Add grated beet mixture. Heat to boiling and ladle into bowls. A heaping tablespoon of cold sour cream may be used to top each serving, but the Russian way is to thin the sour cream with a little of the hot soup and then add it to each serving. Boiled potatoes or *piroshki* may be served with the *borsch*. Makes 4 to 6 servings.

PIROSHKI

(*Savory Filled Pastries*)

Pastry Dough

    1   cup sifted all-purpose flour
    ⅛   teaspoon salt
    ¼   pound butter
    3   tablespoons sour cream

Combine flour and salt, sift into bowl, and cut in butter to size of peas. Add sour cream and stir with fork to form a ball of dough. Wrap in waxed paper and chill 1 hour or longer.

To roll out, divide dough in half and roll each portion into a 9 x 12-inch rectangle, a little less than ⅛ inch thick. Cut each rectangle into twelve 3-inch squares or rounds, or into twelve 2 x 4-inch ovals. Place rounded teaspoonful of filling in center and fold over to make triangles, half moons, or boat shapes, moistening edges with water before pinching together. Chill ½ hour before baking.

Meat Filling

2	teaspoons butter or margarine
3	tablespoons finely chopped onion
¼	pound ground beef
1	tablespoon minced fresh parsley
¼	teaspoon salt
	pinch freshly ground black pepper
1	hard-cooked egg, chopped

Melt fat in skillet, sauté onion, add ground beef crumbled in small pieces. Cook until lightly browned, add remaining ingredients, blend well and cool.

To bake *piroshki*, brush with lightly beaten whole egg that has been mixed with one teaspoon water. Bake 20 minutes or until golden brown at 375 degrees. Serve hot, with soup or as a cocktail accompaniment. (Unbaked *piroshki* may be frozen and baked unthawed.) Makes 24 *piroshki*.

BEEF STROGANOFF

1	pound sirloin or other tender beef filet, free of fat and gristle
	salt and pepper
2	tablespoons butter
1	medium onion, finely chopped
1	tablespoon flour
¾	cup beef bouillon
1	teaspoon prepared Dijon mustard
⅓	cup sour cream

Cut beef filet into slices a little less than ½ inch thick. Pound to flatten meat and break fibers. Cut into strips about ½ inch wide and 1½ inches long. There should be about 2½ cups of beef strips. Sprinkle with salt and pepper and let stand ½ hour at room temperature.

Heat 1 tablespoon of butter to sizzling in skillet. Add beef and brown quickly. Remove meat to bowl, add remaining butter to skillet, and sauté onion until golden. Blend in flour, a little beef bouillon, mustard, and remaining bouillon. Cook, stirring, until thickened. Add meat along with accumulated juices. Cover skillet and simmer on low heat 5 to 10 minutes, until meat is tender.

Stir in sour cream, check seasoning, and heat through gently. Serve with buckwheat *kasha* or boiled rice. Makes 3 to 4 servings.

BUCKWHEAT KASHA

1	cup whole or coarsely ground buckwheat groats
1	egg, beaten
2	cups chicken or beef bouillon
¼	cup butter, margarine, or chicken fat
	salt and pepper

In a bowl combine buckwheat and egg. Heat a deep ungreased skillet, add mixture and cook, turning and spreading with wooden spoon, until each grain is dry and separate. Gradually add bouillon and fat. Cover skillet tightly and cook over low flame 15 to 20 minutes, until liquid is absorbed and buckwheat is tender. Add seasoning to taste. Makes 5 to 6 servings.

SIRNIKI

(*Pot-Cheese Croquettes*)

2	eggs
4	tablespoons flour

    ½   teaspoon baking powder
        dash salt
    4   tablespoons sugar
    ½   teaspoon vanilla extract
    1   teaspoon lemon juice
    ½   teaspoon grated lemon rind
    2   tablespoons sour cream
    1   pound pot cheese, farmer cheese, or very dry cottage
        cheese
4 to 5 tablespoons fine dried bread crumbs
        flour, butter for frying, cinnamon, sugar, sour cream

Beat eggs in a bowl, add flour one tablespoon at a time, and beat smooth with wire whisk. Add baking powder, salt, sugar, vanilla, lemon juice, lemon rind, and sour cream. Add pot cheese, blend well, and put mixture through a sieve. Blend in dried bread crumbs. Chill at least one hour.

To shape *sirniki* for frying, sprinkle a little flour on a square of waxed paper, drop a heaping tablespoonful of chilled cheese mixture onto flour, lift corners of waxed paper, and toss to coat cheese lightly with flour. With hands gently shape cheese into a round patty, ½ inch thick and 2 inches in diameter. Repeat.

Heat 2 tablespoons of butter in a frying pan (a Teflon surface is preferable) to just sizzling. Fry *sirniki* quickly to golden brown on both sides. Serve at once sprinkled with cinnamon-and-sugar mixture (1 teaspoon cinnamon to 4 tablespoons sugar) and topped with sour cream. A serving of 2 to 3 *sirniki* makes a light luncheon dish or a hearty dessert following a light meal. Makes 10 *sirniki*.

KLUKVENY KISSEL

(Cranberry Dessert Pudding)

      2   cups cranberries
      1   cup water
   ¾–1   cup sugar
      1   tablespoon cornstarch
      2   tablespoons cold water
          milk or cream

Wash and pick over cranberries, discarding soft or rotten berries. Place 2 cups cranberries and 1 cup water in saucepan. Cover and bring to boil. Boil about 5 minutes or until all berry skins have popped. Put mixture through strainer and discard skins.

Add sugar to purée to give desired sweetness. There should be about 2 cups of purée. Return to saucepan and bring to boil once. Combine cornstarch and cold water and blend smooth. Add to cranberry mixture. Bring to boil once more, stirring. Cool slightly. Pour into four or five dessert dishes and chill. Serve topped with cream or milk. Makes 4 to 5 servings.

INDEX

ABOUT THE AUTHOR

LILA PERL's interest in regional cuisines has taken her to many countries. Extensive travel through the United States with her husband—also a free-lance writer—provided the inspiration for her first book for World, *Red-flannel Hash and Shoo-fly Pie: American Regional Foods and Festivals.* Her book *Rice, Spice and Bitter Oranges: Mediterranean Foods and Festivals* took her to Portugal and Spain, Italy, Greece, Turkey, Syria, and Lebanon, Israel, Egypt, and Morocco. *Foods and Festivals of the Danube Lands* took her on a delightful trip to the countries touched by the Danube, where she enjoyed delving into the historical past and the colorful present of these tradition-rich lands. Collecting recipes wherever she went, she received a special welcome in Yugoslavia, where many relatives of her husband, Charles Yerkow, still live. Preparing delectable dishes of many lands for her husband and their two children has given Lila Perl, a trained home economist, an expertise that she now shares with her readers. It is her hope that her books will provide culinary inspiration and insights into the cultures of many lands through a greater understanding of their foods and festivals. Lila Perl holds a B.S. degree in Home Economics and has done graduate work in foods at Pratt Institute, New York University, and Columbia University. She and her family live in Beechhurst, New York.

ABOUT THE ILLUSTRATOR

LEO GLUECKSELIG, whose lighthearted drawings festoon this book, has many memories of the lands along the Danube. He was born in Vienna, where he was later graduated from the Academy of Applied Arts. With his wife and young daughter, he now lives in New York City, where he is active in every phase of applied graphics in addition to book illustration.

I   2   3   4   5   73   72   71   70   69

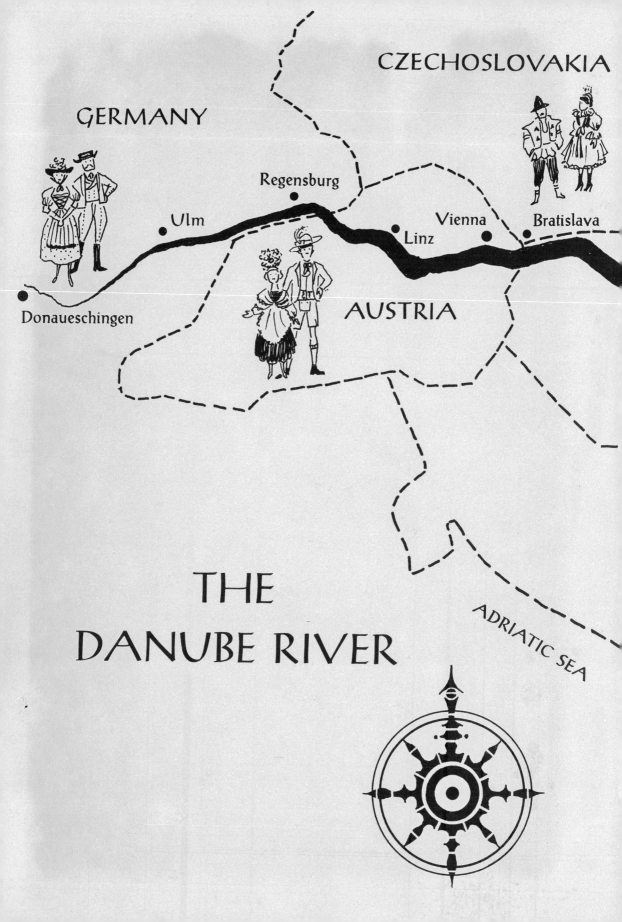

CZECHOSLOVAKIA

GERMANY

Regensburg

Ulm

Vienna

Linz

Bratislava

Donaueschingen

AUSTRIA

THE
DANUBE RIVER

ADRIATIC SEA